United States Presidents

George Washington

Series Consultant:
Don M. Coerver, professor of history
Texas Christian University, Fort Worth, Texas

Wendie C. Old

Enslow Publishers, Inc.

40 Industrial Road	PO Box 38
Box 398	Aldershot
Berkeley Heights, NJ 07922	Hants GU12 6BP
USA	UK

http://www.enslow.com

Library of Congress Cataloging-in-Publication Data

Old, Wendie C.
 George Washington / Wendie C. Old
  p. cm. — (United States presidents)
 Includes bibliographical references (p.) and index.
 Summary: Explores the life and political career of George Washington from his childhood in Virginia, through his role in the American Revolution, to his years as President.
 ISBN 0-89490-832-4
 1. Washington, George, 1732–1799—Juvenile literature. 2. Presidents—United States—Biography—Juvenile literature. [1. Washington, George, 1732–1799. 2. Presidents.] I. Title. II. Series.
 E312.66.043   1997
 973.4'1'092—dc20
 [B]   96-43571
                                              CIP
                                              AC

Contents

1

THE MAN WHO REFUSED TO BE KING

E arly in April 1789, a fifty-seven-year-old man waited on a plantation in northern Virginia. Every day he went about the daily business of running his huge farm. Each evening as he relaxed before the fire, he expected to be notified of the official results of an election being counted in the new United States capital—New York City.

This was an experiment in a brand-new type of national election. By casting their vote, these electors would be choosing a ruler for a new country. This ruler was not to rule for life like a king or emperor. No, for the first time in the history of the world, this ruler would have to face reelection in four years.

The man awaiting the news was George Washington. All signs pointed to his being the person chosen to be the new President. He worried about his ability to govern. He wrote in his journal that his mind was "oppressed with more anxious and painful sensations than I have words to express."[1] Yet he was willing to serve because it would be for the good of the country.

Many people had assumed that after the British had been defeated by Washington's army, he would naturally want to become king of the United States of America. In fact, in 1782 Colonel Lewis Nicola wrote to his commander in chief, General George Washington. He urged Washington to seize power and declare himself king.

Washington rejected the idea with scorn and contempt.[2] His response to Nicola's letter assured him that, ". . . you could not have found a person to whom your schemes were more disagreeable."[3] Nicola apologized.

On April 6, 1789, the electoral votes were counted in the new capital of New York City before the new Congress. Each elector had voted for the two people he thought would make the best President. It was unanimous. Every single elector cast one of his two votes for George Washington. The person with the second highest number of votes, John Adams, became the Vice President of the new United States.

The official results reached Mount Vernon on April 14. Two days later, Washington traveled south to Fredericksburg, Virginia, to say good-bye to his mother. She was slowly dying of breast cancer. He left the management of his estate in the good hands of his nephew, George Augustine Washington.

Although Washington was a rich landowner, he had very little cash on hand. His money was tied up in land and the equipment to run it. He had to borrow money for the trip before he could set off in a well-packed coach drawn by four horses.[4] His wife, Martha, would follow later.

It took eight days to travel from Mount Vernon in northern Virginia to New York City. The coach had no springs to make the ride smoother. It bounced and

Mary Washington's house in Fredericksburg, Virginia, was built on a town lot George Washington inherited from his father. He said his final good-bye to her at this house before he set off to become President of the new United States. She died of cancer during his first term of office.

bumped over the rutted dirt, gravel, oyster shells, and sometimes cobblestone roads.

The long trip northward became a triumphal procession from town to town. Even between the settlements, he was delayed by people running out onto the road to hand him flowers. Others hailed him to offer their good wishes. At times, huge crowds gathered to cheer their adored leader as he rode by. They hung banners and held parades. They saluted him with fireworks or bursts of gunfire and cannon fire. They toasted him at dinners in his honor. Notes in his journal indicate he grew concerned that the people were putting too much faith in him.

The ceremony that affected him the most was held just over the Delaware River from Philadelphia, in the small town of Trenton, New Jersey. This was the site where his frostbitten troops in 1776 had attacked British forces after crossing the Delaware on a cold Christmas morning during the American Revolution.

Today he was offered a seat on a white horse standing on a bridge over Assunpink Creek. Thirteen cloth-wrapped arches shaded him, one for each state in the new union. Thirteen girls sang and spread flowers. Later that evening he wrote that he had been "stirred . . . deeply" by the comparison between this day and that cold winter's battle so long ago.[5]

He was received in the same way throughout New Jersey until he reached the port town of Elizabeth. There he boarded a decorated barge especially built for the occasion. It was manned by thirteen master pilots in white sailor costumes. Ships decorated with flags followed it. One was filled with singers to serenade him. A battery of cannon on Staten Island announced his coming up the Hudson River with a thirteen-gun salute.

He landed at the foot of Wall Street. Here the New York governor, George Clinton, along with a packed crowd greeted him. It was a lot of fuss over one man, but people insisted, "Well, he deserves it all."[6]

Washington was pleased by the display of boats.[7] The crowds cheered and cannons roared to celebrate his arrival.

He settled into the temporary President's House on Cherry Street. He received many visitors during the next week and made calls himself upon officials and friends.

Washington awoke on a clear and mild April 30 Inauguration Day to hear a thirteen-cannon salute. Just after noon, he buckled on his dress sword. He entered an elegant coach pulled by four horses. A short parade up Queen Street ended at Federal Hall where the Congress of the new United States met.

Since that day, American Presidents and Vice Presidents always wear clothing made in America—at least to their inauguration. This tradition began on this day in 1789 when Washington dressed in American-made clothing. His brown coat was made in Massachusetts. His knee breeches were made in Connecticut, as were his white silk stockings and shoes with silver buckles. The buttons on his coat flashed patriotic American eagles.

The joint House of Representatives and Senate members invited Washington into the second floor Senate chamber. Vice President John Adams, who had been sworn into office earlier, greeted him. Then he officially introduced George Washington to Congress.

Next, they moved to the balcony overlooking Wall and Broad Streets. The huge crowd gathered outside would witness his swearing in as President. People jammed the streets below, crowded nearby windows, and even perched on the rooftops.

As no federal judges had been appointed, none were available to swear Washington in. The chancellor of the state of New York, Robert R. Livingston, administered the oath of office. Luckily for the crowd viewing the oath taking, both Livingston and Washington were tall men. Unfortunately, the gentleman holding the Bible was a very short person. He was hidden behind the balcony railing. While Livingston read the oath to him, Washington placed one hand on the Bible open to the book of Psalms and raised the other.

"Do you solemnly swear that you will faithfully execute the office of President of the United States and will, to the best of your ability, preserve, protect, and defend the Constitution of the United States?"[8]

Washington repeated the oath. As he bent to kiss the Bible after taking the oath, he added, "So help me God."[9] (All Presidents since then have added those last

George Washington was sworn into office on April 30, 1789.

SOURCE DOCUMENT

Fellow Citizens of the Senate
and
of the House of Representatives.

Among the vicissitudes incident to life, no event could have filled me with greater anxieties than that of which the notification was transmitted by your order, and received on the fourteenth day of the present month:— On the one hand, I was summoned by my Country, whose voice I can never hear but with veneration and love, from a retreat which I had chosen with the fondest predilection, and, in my flattering hopes, with an immutable decision, as the asylum of my declining years: a retreat which was rendered every day more necessary as well as more dear to me, by the addition of habit to inclination, and of frequent interruptions in my health to the gradual waste committed on it by time.— On the other hand, the magnitude and difficulty of the trust to which the voice of my Country called me, being sufficient to awaken in the wisest and most experienced of her citizens, a distrust

ful

George Washington's Inaugural Address was read to the joint session of Congress directly after his inauguration in New York City.

four words to the oath.) The short attendant raised the Bible as high as he could. However, the first President, who was over six feet tall, still had to bend in order to kiss the Holy Book with his lips.

Livingston presented the new President to the crowd by shouting, "It is done. Long live George Washington, President of the United States."[10] The crowd roared with approval. Cannons boomed in the harbor. Church bells rang.

The group reentered the Senate chamber. Washington then read his short twenty-minute inaugural address in a slow, sometimes trembling voice. It often became too low for anyone to hear.

After a service at St. Paul's church and a private dinner, Washington and his friends toured the city. They appeared at two receptions. They viewed the public fireworks and illuminations, skyrockets, and cannons. The people of the city celebrated in their homes and in taverns with music and laughter.

Throughout the days to follow, Washington was constantly aware that his presidency was a new experiment in democracy. Much of what he would do during the next eight years had never been done before. He knew he was forging a path for others to follow. He said, "I walk on untrodden ground. There is scarcely any part of my conduct which may not hereafter be drawn into precedent."[11]

2

YOUTH

H istory books say that George Washington was born February 22, 1732. However, George Washington always preferred to celebrate his birthday on February 11.[1] That is because the date shown on the calendar in use when he was born was February 11, 1731. This calendar was the old Julian calendar set up by the Roman emperor, Julius Caesar, in 46 B.C.

By the 1700s the Julian calendar no longer matched the seasons of the year. To correct the error the British Parliament adopted the more accurate Gregorian calendar in 1750. By this time George was nineteen years old.

This new calendar shifted many dates by eleven days, including his birthday. In addition, the Julian calendar had begun each new year on Lady's Day in March. The new calendar began the year in January. Therefore, anyone born between January and Lady's Day in March had their birthdays changed by eleven days plus one whole year. George's new birth date became February 22, 1732.

George was born in Westmoreland County, Virginia, at Pope's Creek plantation. The house stood on a point of land sticking out into the south side of the Potomac River.

The Washington family had lived in this area since the mid-1650s. About 1656 his great-grandfather, John Washington, sailed his ship to the American colonies.

Shown here is the front of the replica house at George Washington's Birthplace National Park. (The original was destroyed by fire in 1779.) Historians are not sure exactly how the house looked. This is a typical tidewater Virginia house of that time period.

He intended to buy a load of tobacco to sell in England. Unfortunately, his ship sank. He was forced to stay in Virginia.

George had two older half brothers, Lawrence and Augustine, Jr. Friends and neighbors called Augustine, Sr., by the nickname Gus. Augustine, Jr., was called Austin.

After Lawrence's and Austin's mother died, Gus Washington married Mary Ball. They had many children. George was the oldest of this second group of children. Only five children survived to become adults— George, Betty, Samuel, John Augustine (known as Jack), and Charles Washington.

George was not named after the current king of England, George III, ruler of England, Scotland, Wales, and the colonies, including Virginia. Instead, he was named after the lawyer, George Eskridge, who had raised young Mary Ball when her parents died.

Gus Washington owned six pieces of property in Virginia. His main crop was tobacco for sale to England. He also grew English peas and wheat, plus Native American corn, beans, and pumpkins.

However, most of his income came from the iron mine he owned. This mine located in Stafford County, Virginia, a few miles from the Potomac River. He spent several days a week there, overseeing the works.

When George was three, the family moved upstream to the Epsewasson plantation at Little Hunting Creek.

Young tobacco plants grow at Pope's Creek plantation (George Washington's birthplace) today. Pope's Creek was a working tobacco farm near the mouth of the Potomac River.

The small house on the property contained four rooms opening into a hall, plus a half-story attic for sleeping. They had few neighbors, except for a Native American village across the river. They did have a breathtaking view of the Potomac River from the hilltop, however.

The family moved again in 1738 when George was seven. Taking twenty of their slaves, they settled at Ferry Farm across the Rappahannock River from Fredericksburg. This had the advantage of being both closer to the iron mine and to a town. No longer would Mary Washington have to send shopping orders for clothing and furniture to England by way of a passing ship. Now she could shop right across the river.

Each time the family moved, Gus Washington left

capable overseers to run the other farms. He spent a lot of time riding from plantation to farm to the iron mine, checking on his businesses.

George did not know his father very well. Gus had been away from home more often than he had been home. George remembered him as a tall, fair, kind man.[2]

Although his older brothers were sent to school in England, George was not. Gus Washington died in 1743 before George was old enough to go. When his father died, George was eleven years old. He inherited Ferry Farm, ten of his father's forty-nine slaves, and three town lots in Fredericksburg.

Austin inherited Pope's Creek plantation, including the slaves and livestock. He immediately moved there to live.

Lawrence inherited the water mill, the ironworks, a piece of land near Pope's Creek, and Epsewasson at Little Hunting Creek, along with the slaves working at these places. He remembered how fond George was of Little Hunting Creek. He invited George to visit often. George visited both his brothers whenever he could, but spent more time with Lawrence than with Austin.

Lawrence changed Epsewasson's name to Mount Vernon to honor Admiral Edward Vernon. Lawrence had served under him in the West Indies.

George was too young to inherit property legally. His mother stood as a guardian for him. She was the one who decided they could not afford to send George to school so far away. He attended the local school for young men.

He wrote in his school notes that "America is bounded on ye East with ye Atlantick Ocean. . . . On the West with ye Pacifick South Sea, on the North without Bounds, and on the South with the Magellanick Sea."[3] His spelling was average for the education at that time. However, he was good in math. He also joined his friends for a game of billiards, playing cards, or racing around the countryside on horseback in fox hunts.

George took advantage of Lawrence's invitations to visit Mount Vernon often. He came to look upon Lawrence as a substitute father. Lawrence's tales about the British navy gave George an idea. He decided to run away to sea as a cabin boy at age fourteen.

His mother opposed the idea. Even when Lawrence came down from Mount Vernon to help him plead his cause, George's mother remained firm. She told him he had to stay in school until after he was fifteen years old.

Meanwhile she wrote to her brother, Joseph, in England. His reply came by ship three or four months later and reinforced her decision. He wrote that the British seamen were treated worse than dogs. They were paid poorly and had little chance for advancement unless they had money and connections.

He went on to advise that if George were industrious, he could become a successful planter in the colonies. Planters were the upper-class families who owned vast amounts of land. This group became powerful in the local military and government.

Did George Washington toss a silver dollar over the Rappahannock River? What about the cherry tree? Did George Washington cut down his father's cherry tree and confess because he always told the truth?

Most modern historians believe these were stories made up by Parson Mason Weems, one of the first biographers of George Washington. He published *The Life and Memorable Actions of George Washington* in 1800. Weems created these stories in an attempt to make this private, dignified person seem more human.

A view of one of the remaining outbuildings at Ferry Farm. George Washington studied surveying and kept his surveying supplies here. The rock-lined hole in front of the outbuilding is assumed to be the ice house or the root cellar.

Very little is known about George Washington's childhood. He probably enjoyed most of the activities of a normal boy growing up on a large farm in the British colonies in America. He played in the woods near Little Hunting Creek. He learned how to run Ferry Farm as he grew older. In addition, with Lawrence and Austin away busy running their own plantations, he carried all the responsibilities of being the oldest child of a large family.

His education included the study of a code of honor for a gentleman. This code determined the morals, manners, and other things necessary for an eighteenth-century Virginia gentleman. He learned the proper way to address a member of the aristocracy. This is when he learned that truth was more respected than lies.

George transcribed into his copybook things he wished to remember from his classes. Many of them were from the classic *Rules of Civility and Decent Behavior in Company and Conversation.*[4] This book was created by French priests to make children aware of the effect their behavior had on others. It was used by teachers of many other countries at that time, including Great Britain and the colonies.

Some of these rules talked about being clean and neat in appearance. Others instructed how to act in company: "neither lie nor flatter, do not laugh or talk too loudly, . . . control your temper, . . . listen attentively when in conversation. . . ."[5]

This study ingrained a moral code in him, becoming

SOURCE DOCUMENT

A page from George Washington's copybook. You can see the writing from the back side of the page bleeding through. Students in George Washington's day would copy things from other books that they wanted to keep into their journals. It helped them also to practice their handwriting.

his view of right and wrong. He remained considerate, generous, and true to this code of honor all his life.[6]

George's love of math led him to his first job. He became a surveyor. As more and more people bought land and moved to the colonies, they wanted a record of their boundaries. Fortunes in Virginia were calculated in acres of tobacco instead of pounds of gold. An exact calculation was necessary.

Surveyors used special tools to discover the exact boundaries of properties. Their records were then deposited in a safe place and used to prove who owned which pieces of land.

After George turned sixteen, he lived with Lawrence at Mount Vernon. The estate needed to be surveyed. This allowed George to practice before he attempted to work for other people. The very first piece of ground he surveyed was his brother's turnip field.

Lawrence's wife, Anne, came from English aristocracy. Her father, Colonel William Fairfax, treated George like a son and introduced him to the local high planter society. In 1748, Anne's cousin, Lord Fairfax, hired George to survey lands he had bought. They were located in western Maryland in the Shenandoah Valley, west of the Blue Ridge Mountains. Lord Fairfax, one of the largest and most powerful landowners in Virginia, owned practically all of northern Virginia at that time.

It was an adventurous trip. They traveled in a group led by George's friend, George William Fairfax, the colonel's son. Washington noted in his journal that he

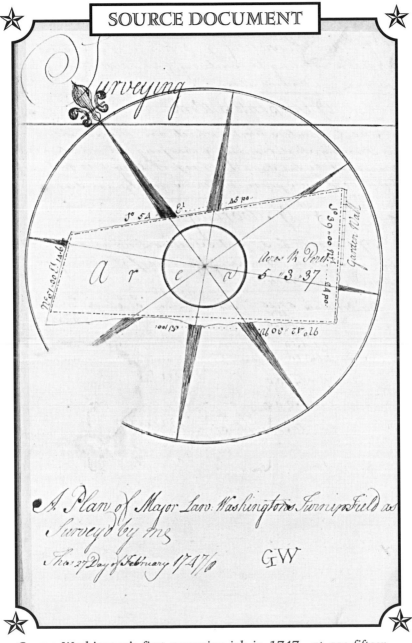

George Washington's first surveying job in 1747—at age fifteen— was to measure his brother Lawrence's turnip field.

often slept under "one thread Bear blanket with double its Weight of Vermin. . . ." such as lice and fleas.[7]

He met German settlers who were living on Fairfax land. They seemed to him to be quite ignorant. They could not even speak English![8]

As payment, Lord Fairfax gave him five hundred acres of Shenandoah land.

In 1749 he became the official surveyor for Culpeper County. With the income from this job, he bought fifteen hundred acres of land in the Shenandoah Valley. He planned to make a profit selling parcels of this land to pioneers who made it across the Blue Ridge Mountains.

His surveying business prospered. He not only worked for the government of the colony but also for many landowners.

Lawrence became sick with a lung disease called tuberculosis in 1751. Many cures were sought, but nothing worked. Finally he and George traveled to the island of Barbados in the Caribbean to see if the milder climate there would help. While on the island, George caught smallpox.

At that time, smallpox was a dangerous disease. It killed most of its victims. Those who survived the attack lived with ugly holes and scars on their face and body called pockmarks. George almost died. He recovered after being sick a long time. Luckily for him, the pockmarks on his face were small, barely noticeable.

George left Lawrence in Barbados. This was the only

George Washington surveyed Natural Bridge, in Virginia, for Lord Fairfax. Several of his surveyor's marks still can be seen there. He climbed twenty-three feet up the southeast wall and chiseled his initials, G.W., into the rock face.

trip George Washington made away from the continent of America.

Lawrence never recovered. He returned home and died in July 1752. George had lost a substitute father, a guardian, a brother, and a friend. He rented Mount Vernon from Lawrence's wife. Some time later, Anne died. George finally inherited his beloved Mount Vernon, which he affectionately called his "home house." At that time it included twenty-five hundred acres as well as eighteen slaves. He lived there for the rest of his life.

Washington also inherited his brother's appointment as adjutant of the Northern Neck district of Virginia in charge of militia training. Suddenly he had become a major in the militia. This post brought a salary of one hundred pounds a year—about $150 in today's money. However, in the 1750s it was an adequate year's salary. It covered the cost of several uniforms for him, plus spending money.

At almost twenty-one years old, Washington's six-foot two- or three-inch-tall body towered over most men. His years as a surveyor had given him a strong body, confidence in himself, and a healthy, outdoors look.

George Washington ran a successful surveying business and owned five thousand acres of land throughout Virginia. To this point, he had survived malaria, smallpox, and pleurisy (a painful inflammation of the diaphragm). He had also traveled in the wilderness and overseas. His schooling and surveying had taught him to write a letter with reasonable penmanship. He had learned how to compute math. Now he had a commission in the armed forces. George Washington was ready to "push his Fortune in the Military Way."[9]

3

SKIRMISHES IN LOVE AND WAR

George Washington fell in love several times. He wrote awkward poetry to his first love while he was still a teenager. Unfortunately, he spent most of his time in strictly male company out in the wilderness on surveying trips. This made him somewhat stiff and awkward with the opposite sex.

He proposed marriage to several young women. In 1751, when he was twenty, he fell in love with sixteen-year-old Betsy Fauntleroy. She was a daughter of a justice of the peace. Her father was also a member of the Virginia House of Burgesses. No matter how many times George asked her to marry him, she refused.

In 1753, Washington was officially commissioned as a major in the colonial Virginia militia by Acting Governor Robert Dinwiddie in the capital of

Williamsburg. His first mission was to take a message to the French.

At that time, Virginia claimed most of the area called the Ohio Territory. It was later called the Northwest Territory. (Massachusetts and Connecticut also claimed parts of that area.) The French from the area now called Canada were invading this territory.

At first French fur trappers and traders floated up and down the rivers. Then the French built forts in the area. Eventually they had forts all along the major rivers. Their forts began at the Saint Lawrence River. Their southernmost fort was situated at their new town of New Orleans located where the Mississippi flows into the Gulf of Mexico.

Governor Dinwiddie, an elderly Scotsman, sent Washington with a few men to confront the French force at Fort Le Boeuf near Lake Erie. His job was to warn the French away from the Ohio Territory. It took him from October 1753 until January 1754 to make the trip there and back.

At one point in the journey, he attempted to cross a river covered with ice. Unfortunately, the ice was not solid. He and his friend fell in the water. By the time they reached shelter, his friend had frostbite, but Washington did not even catch a cold.

Unfortunately, the French refused to budge. They responded by building another fort at a spot called the Forks. It was situated where the Allegheny River joins the Monongahela River to form the Ohio River. The city of Pittsburgh, Pennsylvania, sits there today. The French called their settlement Fort Duquesne.

Governor Dinwiddie promoted Washington to lieutenant colonel in March 1754. Washington then moved with a force of about three hundred men to make Fort Duquesne a British fort.

There was no road between the settlements in Virginia and Fort Duquesne. Washington had to bring along woodcutters to remove trees in the path of his supply wagons. They progressed slowly along this rough trail. In May 1754, his force had arrived within fifty miles of Fort Duquesne.

Washington's spies discovered a small group of French soldiers approaching their camp. On May 28, a small force under Washington's command attacked this French group. His men killed the French commander. In a letter to his brother he described the thrill of his first battle: "I heard the bullets whistle, and, believe me, there is something charming in the sound."[1]

As a result, a strong force of French soldiers and their Native American allies boiled out from the fort searching for him. Washington's men quickly had to throw up a stockade to defend their encampment. They called it Fort Necessity. A stockade is a solid wooden fence made up of rough-cut small trees placed side by side for protection. Holes cut in the stockade allowed the soldiers to fire their guns through it.

Nine hundred French and Native American forces found and attacked them in a driving rainstorm on

July 3.[2] Washington lost over a third of his troops. The French force overran the hastily built fort. Washington had to admit defeat and request surrender terms.

Unfortunately, Washington's translator did a very poor job. The surrender papers included a statement that Washington had fired on French officers while they had been under a flag of truce. The translator also confused the French word for assassination with the word for death. As a result, when Washington signed the surrender, he was also signing an admission that he had murdered (assassinated) the men who had died in the first skirmish.

The remaining troops were allowed to retreat back down the path they had struggled so hard to cut. This left the French in control of the Ohio Territory.

This is Washington's only recorded surrender as a military commander. He learned from the experience.

This battle sparked the conflict known in America as the French and Indian War (1754–1763). The old hatred between France and Great Britain grew hot again. The French used Washington's admission of guilt when they officially declared war on Britain. In Europe the war was called the Seven Years' War (1756–1763).

For two years an undeclared war between Native Americans and the British colonists living near French forts existed. (The six Native American nations of the Iroquois declared their neutrality.) Benjamin Franklin urged the colonies to unite, facing this French threat together. But nothing came of his attempt at this time.

Contra .... C ⁹⁰

1755		
	By Sum brought forward	411.. 16. 1½
	By Cash to my Bro. John suppos'd to be as they were } 5 dubloons	21. 13-4
May 28	By a large Bay Horse of Samᵈ MᶜRoberts	10 __ 6
29	By Phinas for a Bell	0.. 5-9
	By Ditto gave	11.. 6
	By Ropes &c	5 ---
June 1	By altering my Calese	__ 1-3
2	By Captain Ormes Servant	__ 1.3
3	By Cresaps accᵗ	2. 16.10
7	By Mʳ Shirley's Servant	__ 1-3
10	By John Alton	__ 10 __
	By making a black Stock	__ 4 __
	By Cash gave to	__ 5 __
13	By Washing	__ 10.3
	By Thoˢ Phinas	2. 10½
17	By Colº Burton's Servant	2. 10½
27	By Cleaning my Pistols	3. 1½
July 2	By 8 days attendance of a Nurse in my Sickness	8 __
4	By Milk	5. 9
	By 3 pair Hopples	9 -
21	By Mʳ Hawthorn for a Mattress	1. 2.6½
22	By Washing	5-9
	By Thomas Phinas for a Horse	2. 1.6
	By Joseph Bunnian - Batman	5-9
	By Smith for Shoeing my Horse	1-3
23	By Expences at MᶜCrackens	5-9
24	By Jos. Oliver	5-4
	By Expences at Winchester	2.6
	By Ditto at Edward Thompsons	5-9
27	By Water Mellons	1-3
31	By 40 Bushels of Oats	2. __
Augᵗ 1	By Mʳ Posey	4. 6-8
	By my Brothers Serᵗ 1/3. By Besley in fd 96/3	7. 6
	By Mʳ Dalton for Paying Bell & Meads accᵗ	4. 6-0
	By Sum carried Over	£466..12. 3½

George Washington wrote this list of expenses as an officer during the French and Indian War.

Washington became disgusted with British regulars in the army. British soldiers of lower rank than Washington claimed to be superior because they were British, not colonials, and because they had royal commissions, not colonial commissions.[3] He resigned his commission when he arrived home from the disaster at Fort Necessity.

He tried several times to protest this treatment of him by lower ranking royal officers. He made trips to Boston and New York to petition the royal governors there. During one trip, he fell in love. Mary Philipse, age twenty-six, was the daughter of a wealthy landowner. He may have been in love with her inheritance of fifty-one thousand acres.[4] Although he had planned to quickly return home, he stayed in New York City for several weeks to court her. He failed. She also refused to marry him.

In 1755, he was persuaded to rejoin the military as aide-de-camp to General Edward Braddock. He agreed to go as a volunteer, not a soldier. The general and his troops had been sent by Great Britain as one part of a four-pronged effort to remove French influence from the western area of the British colonies. General Braddock planned to attack and capture Fort Duquesne. He needed Washington's first-hand experience.

Washington's mother kept in touch with him even when he was camping in the wilderness. She sent letters complaining that he was neglecting her welfare. At this time most women had no right to run their own affairs.

Washington owned Ferry Farm as well as Mount Vernon. He also owned the house and land in Fredericksburg where his mother later lived.

Although his mother had the use of the house and the income from Ferry Farm, Washington had the final say on the management of the income. If his mother wished to spend more than she had been allowed, Washington had to authorize her requests. In the middle of the harsh rigors of army camp life, he received letters from her. Even when Washington was suffering from an attack of typhoid fever, the letters came. The letters requested more butter, or a new house servant, or complained of his neglect.

The force of more than one thousand men moved slowly through the forest towards the Forks. General Braddock had expected the French to attack as they crossed the Monongahela River about ten miles from the Forks. However, the French were delayed by problems with their Native American allies. As a result, both forces surprised each other in the woods close to the fort.

The British were unable to form ranks and fire in unison. Instead, the men panicked, firing randomly into the woods. The milling men tripped over each other. The advance party of British soldiers retreated back down the path. They merged into the main group, throwing it into confusion. The more flexible French and Native American forces moved around the edges of the milling British army, surrounding it.

The officers were easy to target in their uniforms, especially those on horseback. Two horses were shot out from under George Washington. Four bullets cut through his coat and one through his hat, narrowly missing him. Toward the end of the battle, General Braddock was shot in the lungs. The British retreated.

General Braddock died during the retreat. The soldiers prevented the Native Americans on the French side from digging up his grave and taking his scalp as a trophy. They ran their supply wagons back and forth over the grave eliminating all signs of burial.

Colonel Thomas Dunbar marched the remaining troops to Fort Cumberland on the Potomac River (near

The dying Braddock is carried away from the battle by his troops. He died soon after. His soldiers buried him. Then they ran their horses and carts over the grave to disguise the burial place.

the current town of Cumberland, Maryland). The group then separated. Colonel Dunbar marched the royal soldiers to their winter quarters near Philadelphia. Washington took the few remaining Virginia militia home.

Again Washington learned from his experience. He learned that the French had won because of their willingness to use flexible tactics. The French had not expected to win against a superior force but had used the confusion of the surprise encounter to push their victory.

Washington returned to Mount Vernon to rest from the effects of typhoid and the battle.

Meanwhile, Virginia now had no trained soldiers to defend it. All the British troops were stationed in Philadelphia. Governor Robert Dinwiddie persuaded the Virginia House of Burgesses to approve enough money to support a regiment of soldiers and several companies of rangers. He offered the title of Colonel of the Virginia Militia with increased pay and control of the selection of officers to George Washington.

Washington's sense of duty forced him to accept the post. He reasoned that if it were "offer'd upon such terms as can't be objected against, it wou'd reflect eternal dishonor upon me to refuse it."[5] Washington ordered a flashy blue dress uniform suitable for the promotion.

One regiment plus a few rangers were entirely too few to defend the whole western area of Virginia against attacks from Native Americans. To lend the illusion of a stronger force, Washington set up some forts along the border.

In 1758, Washington's troops merged with royal troops stationed in Pennsylvania for another assault on Fort Duquesne at the Forks. This time the British took Washington's advice. He had suggested that perhaps brown hunting shirts and leggings would be a more suitable uniform for this wild area than their own red coats.

Again the troops built a road for their train of supply wagons to travel on. When they reached the Forks, they discovered the French had burned and abandoned Fort Duquesne.

It was still a prime area for a fort. The British troops built a new fort there called Fort Pitt (the site of present-day Pittsburgh). It was named after William Pitt, the prime minister of Great Britain, who had ordered the advance. A small Virginia unit stayed to garrison it. Most of the colonial troops returned to their bases.

Although the war had not ended, Brigadier General Washington had finished with war. He resigned from the militia in December 1758. Now he would have time to stay home and improve his beloved Mount Vernon—to become a successful planter. But to be successfully run, inside as well as outside, his plantation needed a mistress.

He found his life mate near Williamsburg early in 1758. Martha Dandridge Custis was the young widow of Daniel Parke Custis. She was only twenty-seven years old. With her two children, Washington would have a ready-made family. She was short (five feet tall), plump, with brown hair, hazel eyes, and small hands. She also was the richest widow in Virginia. When her husband died, she inherited about six thousand acres of land, one hundred slaves, plus other assets.[6]

In July 1758, Washington was elected to the Virginia House of Burgesses. Since this colonial body of lawmakers met in Williamsburg, he visited the wealthy widow often.

Of all the many contenders for her hand, Martha chose the war hero, George Washington. They were married on January 6, 1759. It was a grand affair. Outside, the land sparkled with snow. Inside, Washington's slender six-foot three-inch form sparkled in a suit of blue and silver highlighted with red trimming. He even had gold buckles on his knees.

It proved to be a happy marriage for both of them. She brought her placid, practical nature, common sense, and bubbly friendliness that complemented Washington's quiet dignity. Martha described herself as an ". . . old-fashioned housekeeper, steady as a clock, busy as a bee, and cheerful as a cricket."[7]

Since George and Martha Washington were unable to have children of their own, he adopted Martha's two children, John Parke Custis and Martha Parke Custis. Later, after John Custis had died, George invited John's orphaned children to live with them as well.

Washington had a good head for business. He

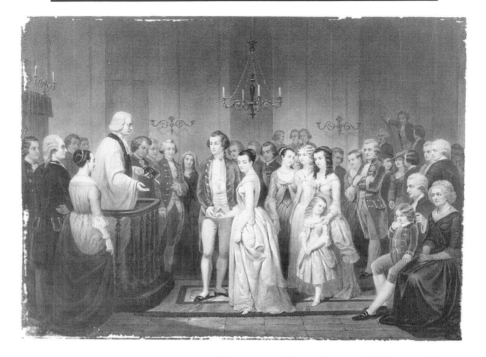

The marriage of George Washington and Martha Dandridge Custis took place on January 9, 1759. (From a lithograph based on a painting by J.B. Sterns.)

understood that he could not raise just one crop and still be successful. Most plantation owners primarily raised tobacco for sale to Europe. Mount Vernon's land was too poor to grow a quality cash crop of tobacco. Therefore, Washington experimented with various other crops to supplement his income. These included Native American corn and wheat as well as foodstuffs. He eventually produced a large quantity of wheat and flour for sale.

He also raised different livestock animals. These fed his ever growing number of workers. They also supplied wool and hides for clothing and for sale. By careful management, he was able to reduce his debt load while nearby plantation owners were getting deeper and deeper in debt.

In a letter to a friend, Washington wrote, "I think . . . that the life of a Husbandman [farmer who also raises animals for sale] . . . is honorable. It is amusing, and, with [good] management, it is profitable."[8]

Slavery was an important part of a successful plantation workforce in those days. Many men and women were needed to plant and harvest, weave and sew, cook and clean. The various additions to the house meant that carpenters and painters were also necessary.

Many of Martha Washington's slaves married Mount Vernon slaves. Washington refused to sell one slave from a family to another owner. It would break up that slave's family unit. He even inserted a clause in his will that all his slaves should be declared free after both he and his wife had died.

Washington improved Mount Vernon in anticipation of living there with his family. The first building period took several years and occurred while he was away at war. The main house was raised to two-and-one-half stories. His friend, William Fairfax, oversaw the construction while Washington was away.

Although the walls look like stone, they actually are large wooden blocks or huge logs grooved to look like stone blocks. Wood was more easily found and transported in that area of Virginia than stone. Sand sprinkled on the wet painted surface adds to the rough,

A close-up of the side of Mount Vernon showing the so-called rusticated boards.

stonelike effect. Washington called the effect rusticated boards.

Washington anticipated nothing more than living the rest of his life contentedly as a busy farmer and a member of the Virginia House of Burgesses. During this time period, he wrote to a friend in England, "I am now, I believe, fixed at this Seat with an agreeable Consort for Life and hope to find more happiness in retirement than I ever experienced amidst a wide and bustling world."[9]

4

THE WAR FOR INDEPENDENCE

Washington the farmer liked British rule just as little as he had when he was a colonial military leader among royal British soldiers. He joined the other men in the Virginia House of Burgesses protesting Britain's colonial policy.

He was, however, not one of the vocal political leaders of the group. He had a violent temper. His temper often was a towering, purple rage.[1] He spent many years learning to keep his temper under control. As a result, he had a habit of thinking long and hard before coming to a decision.

Thomas Jefferson described Washington's debating style as that of speaking briefly and right to the point. The short statements Washington made were respected by the rest of the group.

However, Washington was not yet a rebel. He did not object to British rule of the colonies. He simply objected to certain British government acts that had hit the Virginia plantation owners directly and economically.

The British government had been at war with France off and on for over a century. Each war put the British economy further and further in debt. The latest expensive war with France had put Great Britain even deeper in debt. To help pay for this war, Parliament passed laws taxing British citizens.

Up to this time, the colonies had not paid taxes to Great Britain. Money to pay the royal governors, other government agents, and soldiers had come from taxes in the home country. If the colony needed money to run its government, their own representatives in the House of Burgesses (or other ruling body) would pass the law.

But now, for the first time, the British government decided to tax the colonists. It was about time the colonies supplied the money to support the soldiers who defended them and the officials who governed them.

People who have paid very little in taxes often see any tax increase as a burden. So it was with the colonists. The colonists saw these taxes cutting their already small income down to almost nothing. They also felt the British Parliament had no right to tax the colonies. Only the colonial government had that right.

From 1763 to 1775, the British government attempted to bring the British empire under closer control. In addition, they attempted to improve the collection of taxes. The colonists reacted to each attempt with more and more resistance. At the same time, the British government became more and more determined to make the colonists obey.

Taxes followed taxes. The Navigation Acts were enforced to control smuggling. Taxes on the sugar trade were supposed to raise money to pay for royal troops. Instead they created resentment in the shipping areas of New England. These merchants found smuggling and the sugar trade profitable.

In 1765, the Stamp Act required a stamp on all legal documents, newspapers, playing cards, and dice. Paying for special stamps like these was common in Great Britain. In America the Stamp Act offended lawyers, writers, and gamblers.

The protest came from all parts of the colonies. Patrick Henry proposed a resolution against the Stamp Act in the Virginia House of Burgesses, which brought shouts of "Treason" from some of the other lawmakers. Massachusetts called a Stamp Act Congress. Representatives of nine of the colonies met in New York in October 1765. Their Declaration of Rights and Liberties was sent to Parliament in London, England.

Parliament reacted by repealing the Stamp Act.

In 1767, Charles Townshend became prime minister. The series of acts passed by Parliament under his rule are called the Townshend Acts. In late 1768, British troops arrived in Boston to enforce the acts. Despite the fact that Parliament had passed a Quartering Act, the Bostonians refused to offer the troops any quarters (a place to stay).

In 1769, Washington became a rebel. He was part of the group in the Virginia House of Burgesses who passed a resolution protesting the Townshend Acts. The royal governor disbanded the group. That did not stop the Burgesses. They simply moved the meeting to Willamsburg's nearby Raleigh Tavern.

There Washington introduced several resolutions written by his neighbor George Mason. These resolves insisted that Parliament did not have the right to tax Virginians. They suggested that if people did not import British goods they would not need to pay the taxes. This encouraged colonists in the other colonies to question British authority.

An election in Britain created a new government under Lord North. Most of the Townshend Acts were repealed. The tax on the tea remained. Surely the women of the colonies would insist on continuing to drink their tea. However, the women decided to create new herbal teas rather than pay the tax on tea. Colonists who drank tea were frowned upon.

In 1772, committees of correspondence were formed in most of the colonies. These were groups of men who wrote to each other, keeping each other informed on events in their colony. In this way news traveled quickly from colony to colony. Those who received the news published it in newspapers and broadsides (posters). Resistance to British rule increased. More and more people thought of themselves as Americans instead of as British citizens.

On December 16, 1773, a resistance group called the Sons of Liberty disguised themselves as Native Americans of the Mohawk tribe. They crept aboard ships in Boston Harbor and dumped their cargo of bundles of tea into the water. Washington disapproved of this Boston Tea Party.[2]

The British government retaliated by imposing several Intolerable Acts. These acts closed the port of Boston until the tea was paid for. Another part of the act also ordered the people of Boston to let British troops live in their houses (enforcement of the Quartering Act).

If the British Parliament had hoped Massachusetts would give in because of being isolated from her sister colonies, they were doomed to disappointment. These Intolerable Acts only served to unite the colonies in a way that had never happened before.

Washington joined the men of Virginia and the other colonies who rallied around the colony of Mass-achusetts. In September 1774, a meeting of fifty-five representatives of the twelve colonies was held mid-point up the coast at Philadelphia. (Georgia refused to send a representative.) They called themselves the Continental Congress.

Washington was one of the seven Virginia Burgesses chosen to attend. Others included Richard Henry Lee and Patrick Henry. Washington stayed quietly in the background observing all that went on. However, he wore his military uniforms to the meetings to emphasize his experience as a soldier.

Washington served on various military committees. He even offered to organize a regiment for the group. Other representatives at the Continental Congress, including John Adams and John Hancock, took note of this tall, military man.

At this time, the Congress was not looking for war. They had no intention of becoming independent from Britain. They simply wanted to be treated fairly, with all the rights and privileges of any British citizen. Unfortunately, the British government was not willing to make concessions. In fact, King George III of Great Britain wrote, "the Colonies must either submit or triumph . . ."[3]

In March 1775, Patrick Henry inspired his fellow Virginia legislators to reject moderate action. His speech ended, "I know not what course others may take; but as for me, give me liberty or give me death!"[4]

At that same meeting, Washington again was chosen to be one of the men representing Virginia at the Second Continental Congress in Philadelphia. They were to meet in May.

However, the first military encounter of the American Revolution occurred the month before they met. In April 1775, the British regulars stationed in

George Washington in 1772 in his blue soldier's uniform. He wore the uniform to the meetings of the First and Second Continental Congresses to remind the delegates that he was the only one of them with previous military experience.

Boston fought the colonial irregular militia outside of Boston. This "shot heard round the world" occurred at Lexington and Concord.[5]

What to do about the New England militia army that was besieging the British troops in Boston? The Continental Congress voted to support them. On June 15, 1775, John Adams nominated George Washington to be general and commander-in-chief of the army of the United Colonies. Some of his praise included: "the modest and virtuous, the amiable, generous and brave George Washington Esquire."[6] Washington remained out of the room until the vote had been cast.

The election was unanimous. By choosing a southern commander to lead troops in a northern colony, the Continental Congress would show the world that all the colonies were united in this matter. Washington was forty-three years old. He was in good health. Plus, he had the advantage of previous command experience.

Washington refused a salary. He only asked that his expenses be paid. (Congress did not pay him until after the war.) He confessed later to Martha that, although he did not think he was the best man for the job, he could not refuse. Refusing would have exposed ". . . my character to such censure as would have reflected dishonor upon myself."[7] He would not see his beloved Mount Vernon for another six years.

He and his appointed staff headed north on June 23. When they reached New York City, they learned that the colonial defeat at the Battle of Bunker Hill had taken place in Boston on June 17. However, it was a costly battle for the British. The colonists killed or wounded over 40 percent of the British forces as they retreated from Breed's Hill.

On July 3, 1775, Washington took command of the colonial force besieging Boston. He struggled to transform the ragged group he found there into a real army. He set up a proper siege of Boston.

He sent Benedict Arnold and Richard Montgomery to invade Canada. This action would prevent the British with their Native American allies from attacking from that direction. They also were to invite Canada to become the fourteenth colony. Unfortunately, they were defeated. Arnold was wounded. Montgomery was killed.

Still, the British government did not make any sign of conciliation toward the colonists. In January 1775, Parliament declared the colonists to be in a state of rebellion. They ordered all the ports of the colonies closed. The Continental Congress replied on April 6 by throwing their ports open to all the commerce of the world *except Great Britain*. Then they sent a request to Great Britain's enemy, France, for help.

At last Washington received cannons captured from a British fort at Ticonderoga, south of Lake Champlain. He immediately used them to force the British to evacuate Boston. They left on March 17, 1776, taking with them various loyalist (loyal to the king of England)

The Revolutionary soldiers dressed in a variety of uniforms as illustrated by these reenactors at Washington Crossing State Park.

families who were afraid of retaliation from the victorious rebels.

Washington next moved to defend New York City. He made a quick trip to Philadelphia in June to request money for the troops. However, he was back commanding the troops in New York when Thomas Jefferson and his committee put the Declaration of Independence before Congress for a vote. As a result, Washington's signature is not on this important American document.

On July 2, 1776, the Second Continental Congress formally severed the last tie between America and Great Britain. On July 4, it endorsed the Declaration of Independence. The conflict was now officially a war for independence.

SOURCE DOCUMENT

In CONGRESS, July 4, 1776.

A DECLARATION

By the REPRESENTATIVES of the

UNITED STATES OF AMERICA,

In GENERAL CONGRESS ASSEMBLED.

WHEN in the Courſe of human Events, it becomes neceſſary for one People to diſſolve the Political Bands which have connected them with another, and to aſſume among the Powers of the Earth, the ſeparate and equal Station to which the Laws of Nature and of Nature's God entitle them, a decent Reſpect to the Opinions of Mankind requires that they ſhould declare the cauſes which impel them to the Separation.

We hold theſe Truths to be ſelf-evident, that all Men are created equal, that they are endowed by their Creator with certain unalienable Rights, that among theſe are Life, Liberty, and the Purſuit of Happineſs.

Signed by Order and in Behalf of the Congress,

JOHN HANCOCK, President.

Attest.
CHARLES THOMSON, Secretary.

Philadelphia: Printed by John Dunlap.

The first printed copy of the Declaration of Independence is called the Dunlap Broadside. After it was approved by the Continental Congress, John Dunlap printed copies to be sent to state assemblies, committees of safety, and commanders of the Continental Troops. It was this broadside that George Washington read to his troops.

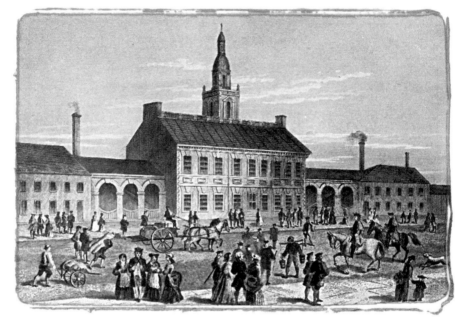

Independence Hall in Philadelphia, Pennsylvania. Philadelphia was a good place for the Continental Congresses to meet because it was the central point among the thirteen colonies.

The world's first submarine attack occurred on September 6, 1776. A Continental soldier, David Bushnell, attempted to sink British Admiral Richard Howe's flagship using his submerged boat, the *Turtle*. He failed.

Washington was unable to hold New York City against the British. In the late fall, the American colonial troops fled across New Jersey with the British army in pursuit. When Washington's army crossed the Delaware into Pennsylvania, just north of Philadelphia, the Continental Congress panicked. They fled to Baltimore.

In late December, the British army declared that the war was over for the season. They settled into campsites for the winter. However, Washington's army recrossed the Delaware on Christmas Day. They attacked the sleeping Hessian mercenaries (paid foreign soldiers) stationed in Trenton, New Jersey. Then Washington moved to drive the British out of Princeton, New Jersey. After this second victory, Washington ordered his own army into winter quarters near Morristown, New Jersey.

Martha Washington came north from Virginia in the family coach to stay with George until spring. She did this during the winter of 1776–1777 and every winter for the rest of the war.

The British spent the summer of 1777 attempting to capture Philadelphia. They finally succeeded on September 26. The Continental Congress retreated even

Emanuel Leutze's famous painting, Washington Crossing the Delaware, *shows Washington fighting broken ice and sleet.*

farther away—to Annapolis, Maryland—and continued to meet.

Meanwhile, several reinforcements arrived from Europe. The Marquis de Lafayette arrived in July from France with a troop of men.

An American force under General Horatio Gates accepted the surrender of British General John Burgoyne at Saratoga, New York, on October 17. The tide turned in favor of the rebels. News of this victory gave France the push it needed to declare itself on the American side. Gates became the hero of the day.

SOURCE DOCUMENT

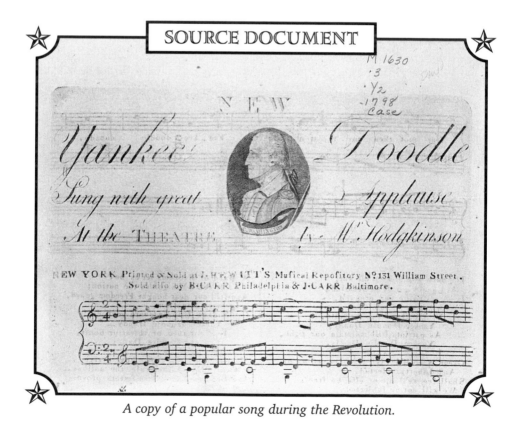

A copy of a popular song during the Revolution.

A group of men plotted to replace Washington with General Gates. However, Congress refused to consider it. They pledged their support to Washington as commander.

Winter quarters in 1777–1778 were established at Valley Forge, Pennsylvania. It was just twenty-five miles northwest of British-held Philadelphia. By this time the troop's uniforms had become quite ragged. Many soldiers quit and returned to their own homes and farms. The ones that stayed shivered under inadequate tents and few blankets. Gradually log shelters were built. (Some of the buildings and earth fortifications can still be seen at Valley Forge National Park.)

Prussian officer Baron Friedrich Wilhelm von Steuben arrived in February 1778. He took charge of training at the winter camp. He instructed the Continental Army troops in European tactics and discipline. Von Steuben was a feisty soldier who would scream, yell, and swear at the troops. When they marched out of camp, the starving, tattered army had been molded into an effective military body.

In June of 1778, the British made their first feeble peace overtures. However, Congress rejected their terms.

In July 1778, representatives in Congress began signing the Articles of Confederation. (They had already voted to change their name from United Colonies to the United States.) It took eleven more months for all the

Washington addresses his ragged troops at Valley Forge. This is a nineteenth-century engraving. One of the people to the left of George Washington is the Baron Friedrich Wilhelm von Steuben.

colony representatives to sign. This agreement formed the colonies into a country of loosely-banded states.

The war continued on other fronts as well. The soldiers under George Rogers Clark plowed through the Northwest Territory. They attacked British forts there. The final victory took place at Vincennes, Indiana, in July.

In September 1779, the Spanish in North America captured British forts along the Gulf of Mexico and the southern Mississippi River. Also in September, Congress authorized John Adams to begin negotiating peace with Britain.

The British continued to harry the new United States with both their navy and army. Their thrust into the southern United States from the sea proved successful. Polish-born Continental Army officer Count Casimir Pulaski was killed in October 1779 in an attempt to recapture Savannah, Georgia, from the British.

Winter quarters at Morristown, New Jersey, (1779–1780) proved to be even worse than those at Valley Forge. The soldiers suffered from a lack of warm clothing and nourishing food. Washington tried to coax and flatter Congress for money to feed, supply, and pay his soldiers. There was never enough.

George Washington's ragged troops used any means possible to keep warm during winter. Reenactors standing by their oars at Washington Crossing State Park illustrate the variety of foot coverings used by colonial soldiers.

In 1780 on the southern front, the United States forces were defeated in Charleston, South Carolina. This was offset by a victory in Springfield, New Jersey, led by General Nathanael Greene. Five thousand French soldiers led by General Comte de Rochambeau arrived to aid the cause in July.

Another major blow to the war came when the commander of West Point, Benedict Arnold, was exposed as a traitor on September 2, 1780. He had been giving American plans to the British since 1779. Arnold fled to a British ship. The British rewarded him with the rank of brigadier general in the British army. He continued to fight—against Washington.

Arnold had been a trusted officer whose wit Washington had enjoyed. The angry Washington shrieked in a black fury at Arnold's betrayal of the American cause.[8]

On the southern front, British General Charles Cornwallis's attempt to invade North Carolina failed. He then sailed up the coast to occupy Virginia. Governor Thomas Jefferson narrowly managed to escape capture.

On March 1, 1781, all the states formally ratified the Articles of Confederation. Maryland was the last state to do so.

Washington and French General Rochambeau then pretended to prepare to attack New York. Moving swiftly, instead they headed south. They combined with French sea forces to attack British General Lord Charles Cornwallis's base at Yorktown, Virginia.

SOURCE DOCUMENT

The Articles of Confederation was drafted in November 1777, completed July 9, 1778, and ratified in February 1781. The articles created a league of friendship between the separate states, not a national government.

On October 19, 1781, Cornwallis surrendered. The largest body of British troops in America had been defeated. However, Cornwallis refused to appear at the surrender ceremony. He sent his second-in-command instead.

During the ceremony, the British military band played a song that expressed their feelings about the great British empire being defeated by a ragged band of rebels—"The World Turned Upside Down." Neither side had achieved a total military victory. However, all were ready for peace.

The surrender at Yorktown as painted by John Trumbull. General Cornwallis refused to appear at the surrender ceremony. As a result, Washington refused to accept the British troops' surrender himself. He sent his second-in-command, General Benjamin Lincoln (on the white horse), to accept the surrender. Washington sits on a dark horse near the American flag.

During 1782, both the invading British troops and thousands of Loyalists fled the country. In France, Benjamin Franklin met with British representatives in Paris to discuss the peace terms. He had to insure that the terms included a provision that the colonies were now a separate country.

Britain gave up all of its territory in America, except Canada, to the newly formed United States. This included the lands west of the mountains where Daniel Boone and George Rogers Clark had been exploring and developing settlements. It extended all the way over to the Mississippi River. However, the borders were vague. For a long time afterwards, the area west of the mountains over to the Mississippi was disputed by Spain and the Canadian (British) fur traders.

Since Britain had been at war with so many countries, it had to sign peace treaties with all of them. In January 1783, the British signed treaties between Great Britain and Spain. This gave Spain rule over East and West Florida plus the land west of the Mississippi River. Another treaty between Great Britain and France recognized British rule in Canada. As soon as the treaty between Great Britain and France was ratified, the American peace treaty went into effect. It was over. No more war.

5

UNDER THE ARTICLES OF CONFEDERATION

T idying up after a war is not easy. The men who fought the war wished to be paid. However, the terms of the Articles of Confederation did not give Congress the power of taxation (the power to raise money for expenses). Only the states had that power. Therefore, they were slow to gather money to pay off the soldiers. Again and again, Washington pleaded for his men.

In March 1783, Washington's officers heard a rumor that Congress was never going to pay them. They threatened to put out a general call to the army not to disband until they were paid.

Washington gathered the officers together. He asked them to have more faith in Congress. He began to read to them a congressman's letter about this matter.

However, he realized he could not read the small print. He paused. Then he took out his reading glasses. He begged their pardon and said, "I have already grown gray in the service of my country. I am now going blind."[1] He was over fifty years old.

He also had been using reading glasses for years. This was just another example of his knack of knowing just the right words to defuse a situation and cause an emotional response. He persuaded them to wait and see what would happen.

This and many other actions caused Washington to be respected by his men and popular with the country-folk. He constantly applied his early training in honor, duty, and fairness to everything he did.

He had not imposed his rule on the army like a dictator. He had relied on his staff for advice and assistance.

Therefore, it came as a surprise when he learned that a group of army men wished him to become king of the United States. He told them in no uncertain terms that he would not do it. He insisted that military rule was the wrong way to govern the country. He insisted on preserving the civil government.

The news that the Treaty of Paris had been signed reached Washington in October 1783. Washington issued his "Farewell Orders to the Armies of the United States." As the men were disbanded in small groups, they were given certificates of service. They were allowed to take their muskets home with them but received no back pay.

After he had accepted the surrender of New York City from the British troops there in December, he gathered his remaining officers for a farewell party at Fraunces Tavern. His toast to them over a glass of wine was a typically short one. He reminded them he was grateful for their services. He wished them prosperity and happiness in the future. As they came forward to shake his hand, Washington embraced them, one and all.

Although Washington felt the United States must maintain an army, even in peacetime, he was determined not to lead it. He could not wait to be home at his peaceful Mount Vernon. When he reached Annapolis, Maryland, where Congress was now in session, he submitted his official resignation. He fully believed this would be the ". . . last solemn act of my official life. . . ."[2]

Thomas Mifflin, then president of Congress, offered the gratitude of the country to Washington. He thanked Washington not only for his splendid achievements but also because he had always obeyed the civil authority.

At last he reached his beloved home. He was in time to celebrate Christmas with Martha and their family.

For the next few years, he worked to get Mount Vernon back on its feet as a successful farm. Because his land was no longer fertile, Washington continued to experiment with crops.

Washington resigning his commission to the Continental Congress at Annapolis, Maryland.

Washington also raised mules. Mules are the offspring of a male donkey and a female horse. They are large and strong. They can pull heavy loads. However, mules cannot reproduce. Therefore, you cannot raise more mules unless you own both donkeys and horses. At this time, most donkeys came from Spain. Spanish law forbade exporting the male donkeys. This meant if a person wanted a mule, he had to buy one from Spain. King Charles III of Spain sent Washington several fine male donkeys for the breeding of the hard-working mules.

Washington continued to enlarge the house at Mount Vernon. At one end he added personal quarters—a bedroom above his study on the first floor. The final enlargement was added to the opposite side of the house. It was a large formal dining room two stories tall.

Washington's mother (Mary Ball Washington) still lived in Fredericksburg, Virginia. Her daughter lived a few blocks away. Mother and son were not on especially good terms. He would visit her occasionally, making certain she did not lack anything. However, he never invited his mother to visit Mount Vernon. She continued to complain to others about his neglect.

Aside from his mother, it often seemed the whole world came to Mount Vernon to visit. Even some of the British officers whom he had fought against visited the plantation. Washington welcomed them all.

Washington's war expenses were eventually paid. He continued to push Congress to pay his soldiers. Finally they were paid—partially in land and partially in paper money. Using his previous surveying experience, he toured the proposed land grants to see that all was in order. He made sure that his men were not going to get shortchanged.

Unfortunately, the paper money that the Continental Congress ordered printed for the new nation had no financial backing. The soldiers discovered it took more paper notes to buy the same amount of goods than it did several years ago. The expression "not worth a continental" became popular. It meant that something was almost worthless.

Economic conditions grew from bad to worse. The Continental Congress under the Articles of

Confederation did not seem to be able to stop the decline. Under the Confederation, the rights and powers of the state were stronger than the rights of the national government.

To many, freedom from Britain's rule meant freedom from any sort of central government rule. The former colonies still did not trust the idea of a central government controlling them.

Congress depended upon the good will of the states for money. It could not tax the people directly. One state could tax their citizens more heavily than another one did. Yet none of the states sent enough of the money

SOURCE DOCUMENT

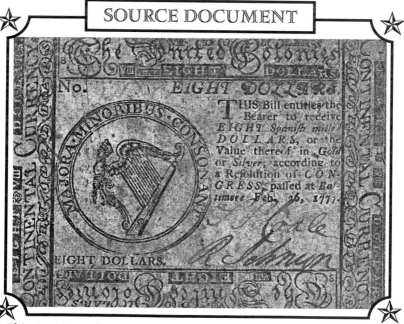

This Continental paper money was worth eight Spanish dollars. The harp has thirteen strings for the thirteen colonies. The Latin inscription, Major Minoribus Consonant, *means the large colonies are in harmony with the small colonies.*

they collected to Congress to support a central government.

The Confederation had very little power over the states. It could only suggest, not force, the states to abide by various resolutions.

Some states issued their own paper money. Although it had little value, the states tried to force merchants and farmers to use it. In 1786, some unhappy Massachusetts farmers took up arms because of heavy taxation and the low value of money. It was called Shays' Rebellion.

The rebelling farmers attempted to prevent the courts from foreclosing their farms because of debt. Poorly armed and organized, they soon fled to the unsettled western lands. Others surrendered when their families began to starve. The news caused Washington to lament, "We are fast verging to anarchy and confusion!"[3]

When Massachusetts asked the Confederation for help to put down this rebellion, Congress could not give any. There was no national army. Congress could not force the other states to help. There was no single President to make decisions. Everything had to be discussed and voted on in Congress.

More people began to talk about the need for a strong central government—possibly even a king.

Washington wrote to his friend (and secretary of foreign affairs), John Jay, "What a triumph for the advocates of despotism to find that we are incapable of governing ourselves. . . ." The two discussed what measures should be taken to avoid this.[4]

Gradually the various states began to see they needed to work together. A meeting of delegates from five states was held at Annapolis, Maryland, in September 1786. It concluded with a resolution offered by Alexander Hamilton and James Madison. It suggested that all thirteen states needed to choose delegates to a convention to correct the problems with the Articles of Confederation.

Congress accepted the Annapolis Convention report. It ordered a Federal Convention to meet at Philadelphia in May 1787. This convention would have the limited purpose of revising the Articles of Confederation.

Only twelve states sent representatives. Rhode Island declined to join. All the delegates had had experience as legislators or teachers. However, the majority were quite young—between thirty and forty years of age. George Washington at fifty-five was among the older statesmen. Benjamin Franklin at age eighty-one was the oldest.

The list included many of the influential political men at that time. John Jay, John Adams, and Thomas Jefferson were out of the country busy with foreign affairs and could not come.

Washington was again one of the delegates from Virginia. He was unanimously elected president of the convention. His diplomatic talents and reputation for dealing fairly with all were desperately needed during the rowdy meetings.

The large states wanted a strong federal government with population being the basis for representation in the legislative body. The small states wanted each state to have an equal vote.

The compromise plan provided for a two-body

George Washington was president of the convention which wrote the United States Constitution. This painting is by Charles Willson Peale.

legislative branch of government. The Senate would have two representatives from each state. The House of Representatives would have its membership based on the number of people in the state.

Eventually the compromises within the convention began to emerge as the basis of the proposed government itself. The President would be elected by the people. He would have the power to balance or veto any rash laws passed by the two legislative houses. However, his power also had checks and balances. He had to have Senate approval of any person he appointed to high office and approval of treaties. Only members of Congress could declare war, not the President. Also, Congress had the power to impeach (charge with misconduct in office) a President.

The judges in the judicial system served as a third check and balance. They would have the power to rule on the decisions of both the President and the legislature.

As President of the convention, Washington could not join the debate. He could, however, control who might or might not speak— and for how long. However, he made his opinions known during the conversations after the meetings were over for the day.

He used his prestige, his commanding tone of voice, and the respect of his fellow men to guide the bickering state representatives into formatting a workable document.

The Constitution avoided the dictatorial rule of

kings by making it clear that the government could peacefully enforce its laws throughout the states. It was also clear that the government's powers were limited to those mentioned in the Constitution itself.

Many people naturally assumed that Washington would be the first President. Therefore, when they debated the powers of the presidency, they often were discussing how Washington, himself, would handle the powers. Benjamin Franklin summed up the convention's feelings this way: "The first man put at the helm will be a good one. . . . nobody knows what sort may come afterwards."[5]

Because he was the president of the Constitutional Convention, Washington had the honor to be the first person to sign the completed document.

The delegates had gone beyond their instructions. Instead of repairing the Articles of Confederation, they had junked it. They had created a whole new type of government.

Before the Constitution could become the law of the land, nine of the thirteen states had to approve it. Back in Virginia, Washington worked hard to ensure his state was among the first to ratify it.

As predicted, many people found things to criticize about it. Patrick Henry thundered, "Your President may easily become a King." He wanted a Bill of Rights added. James Monroe gloomily predicted a President who might be reelected for life.[6]

Defenders of the new Constitution replied that this

The Constitution of the United States was first signed by George Washington. He was president of the Constitutional Convention.

was unlikely. The President could not become a king because the United States had no aristocracy or powerful controlling church to support such a thing. Besides, the President would be elected for a short term. He would have to go back to the people for reelection in four years.

By the end of 1788, the required nine states had ratified it. The path was clear for the first election of an American President.

George Washington did not campaign for the office of President. He was, however, aware his friends were planning to put his name in nomination. The vote was held by the electoral college on February 4, 1789. By this time, eleven states had ratified the Constitution and were allowed to send electors. When Washington was notified that he had been unanimously elected President, he realized he would again have to leave his beloved Mount Vernon to serve his country.

6

FIRST PRESIDENT
OF THE
UNITED STATES

W ashington's first act as President on April 30, 1789, was to present a short (twelve-hundred words) inaugural address to Congress. In it he added his voice to those who wished a Bill of Rights to be part of the Constitution.

Washington was aware his example would set the tone of the government from then on. He told James Madison, "As the first of every thing . . . will serve to establish a Precedent. . . . it is devoutly wished on my part, that these precedents may be fixed on true principles."[1]

One precedent he attempted to set was again to refuse a salary. He asked that his expenses be paid instead. Congress refused his request. They voted the President a $25,000 annual salary.[2]

Since Washington needed to buy everything new to set up the office of President, he often overspent his salary. He made up the difference with income from Mount Vernon. When his salary would not cover the expense of the number of servants Washington felt were necessary, he brought his own up from Mount Vernon.

Fifty-three-year-old John Adams received the second most number of electoral votes. This made him the Vice President. Congress gave him a salary of $5,000. He had little responsibility or power. He governed the Senate. He stood ready to take over as President if the President resigned or died. Adams referred to his job as the "most insignificant office" that had ever been invented.[3]

Washington had at least four goals for his first term in office. One was to preserve the government that represented the people of the United States. The second was to put the finances of the nation on a firm basis by raising taxes and settling debts. The third was to normalize relations with Europe and the British empire. Fourth, he would support the development of the frontier and deal with the Native Americans.

This new government was an experiment with democracy. He found himself the only elected head of a government in the world. He was the President of a weak, agricultural republic facing large, unfriendly monarchies ruled by kings. (Luckily the European monarchies were a six-to-eight-week sail away across the ocean.) The treasury was empty. There were still debts to be paid from both the American Revolution and

One of Washington's objectives was to make treaties with the neighboring Native Americans such as the Mohawks. Shown here is Joseph Thayendaneken, a Mohawk chief.

the previous government under the Articles of Confederation.

He did not see any need for opposing political parties. He gathered men to work under him who held completely opposite views from each other. He chose men simply because he felt they were the best men for the job.

His secretary of the treasury, Alexander Hamilton, advocated a strong central government with strong powers. Hamilton thought the office of the President should dominate Congress and take control of policy-making. He also was in favor of an alliance with the British. Hamilton encouraged the British to invest in American industries.

However, Washington's secretary of state, Thomas Jefferson, disagreed with almost every Hamilton belief. Jefferson had been a governor of the state of Virginia. Naturally he believed in stronger state powers and a weaker centralized government.

In addition, he remembered his experience when he had been ambassador to France. Jefferson had seen the extremely rich ruling classes living in luxury while poor people had only rags to wear and begged for food to eat. He assumed these social conditions were caused by the strong central government there. He feared it might happen here. Washington valued the advice of both Hamilton and Jefferson.

Congress considered many issues during the first year. Among them was the question of how to address

Washington's Cabinet during his first term from left to right: Henry Knox—secretary of war, Thomas Jefferson—secretary of state, Edmund Randolph—attorney general, and Alexander Hamilton— secretary of the treasury.

their executive officer—the President. John Adams, as president of the Senate, wished to have a title for himself. He wanted an even more exotic title for Washington.[4] After all, the rulers of Europe were addressed by titles.

In May of 1789, a congressional committee looking into the matter proposed that the President should be called, "His Highness, the President of the United States of America and Protector of their Liberties."[5]

Congress voted it down. It sounded too much like the way one addressed a king. They decided there would be no special title for the Vice President. The President would be referred to as The President of the United States of America. George Washington was pleased with the decision.[6] This has since been shortened to the term used today—Mr. President.

On June 1, 1789, Washington became the first President to sign an act of Congress into law.

In July, the poor starving people in the cities and countryside of France followed the American colonies' example. They declared a revolution of their own. It began on July 14 with the storming of the Bastille. This fortress contained gunpowder, weapons, and a handful of political prisoners.

A year later, General Lafayette sent the captured key of the Bastille to his dear friend, George Washington, along with a sketch of the fortress he had ordered destroyed. Today they hang together in the central hall of Mount Vernon.

After the French Revolution began, Jefferson was in favor of an alliance with the French rebels. Hamilton preferred joining the British.

At first Washington tried to follow the instruction in the Constitution that said he should negotiate treaties with the advice and consent of the Senate. In August 1789, Washington went to the Senate. He proposed to get advice about a treaty he wanted to make with the Creek and other Native American nations in the south. He brought a list of questions he wanted to discuss.

The senators debated the questions but were unable to reach an agreement that day. They decided to postpone their answer until later.

"This defeats every purpose of my coming here," Washington shouted.[7] He stomped out. From then on, he established the policy of the President negotiating treaties using his own judgment with the advice of his cabinet. He sent the treaties to the Senate for ratification afterwards. Foreign policy was fully in the hands of the President and his cabinet. Another precedent had been set.

During the next few months of 1789, more governmental offices were created in the executive department—Foreign Affairs (now Department of State), the Department of War, the Treasury Department, the National Post Office, and the Judicial Department. The Judicial Department included the attorney general's office and all the various federal courts. The heads of these five departments eventually became what is now known as the President's Cabinet of advisors.

One of the first acts of Secretary of the Treasury Alexander Hamilton was to negotiate a loan to the United States government. He received loans from several New York banks on September 13, 1789. These loans helped to stabilize the money problem. It enabled him to begin building a solid fiscal base for the government. His next step called for taxes to support the ongoing expenses of the government.

Hamilton proposed that the federal government pay off the states' debts left over from the American Revolution. In this way, he could establish the federal government's credit. It would also convince the states to work together to pay off the joint debt.

However, the Constitution had not specifically stated that the federal government could do such a thing. Therefore, Jefferson was against it. Hamilton argued that if the Constitution did not specifically forbid an action, it implied that the action could be done. Jefferson believed the opposite. These two views of the Constitution have been argued about ever since.

Washington's mother was never able to visit New York City to see her son filling the position of President of the United States. On August 25, 1789, she died of cancer.

The judicial arm of the government swung into operation on February 1, 1790, when the Supreme Court held its first session. Washington appointed six judges to this court. He also appointed all the judges for the circuit and federal district courts.

Washington appointed only men of integrity whom he knew or who were recommended by men he knew. No one who was lazy or a heavy drinker was considered. He set a high standard for honesty and efficiency.

He would not appoint any close relations, neither uncles, brothers, nor nephews. He attempted to spread the appointments throughout the regions of the states to keep a balance of power.

Women were not even considered. Neither were Native Americans. No servants or slaves of any race were considered. It would be many years before these groups had any political rights in this new nation.

The last two holdouts of the original colonies finally ratified the Constitution and joined the Union of the United States. North Carolina ratified it on November 21, 1789. Rhode Island joined on May 29, 1790.

In March 1790, the first national census began. It found that approximately 3.9 million people lived in the young United States.[8] Seven hundred thousand of these were slaves or servants.

Where should the new nation's capital be located? Rather than in either the North or the South, a central location was sought.

It was thought a brand-new area should be created for the capital. Washington recommended a piece of land just north of Mount Vernon on the Potomac River.

On July 16, 1790, Congress approved the location.

President Washington signed the plans for the new United States capital district to be called the District of Columbia. Both Virginia and Maryland were supposed to donate equal amounts of land on either side of the Potomac River, making the city ten miles square. However, only Maryland land was finally incorporated into the city.

Three commissioners surveyed the land and planned the city. Pierre L'Enfant, a French architect and engineer who had become a major in the American Revolution, was in charge. His assistants were Andrew Ellicott and Benjamin Banneker, a free African-American mathematician and surveyor.

In December of 1790, the capital was moved from New York City to Philadelphia, the second largest city in the land. The final move to the new capital on the Potomac would not occur until ten years later.

In 1791, the three commissioners announced the city would be named the city of Washington in honor of the President. However, George Washington always referred to it as the Federal City.

To handle treasury matters, Congress chartered the Bank of the United States on February 25, 1791. This fulfilled one of Hamilton's dreams. Again Jefferson disagreed. He thought it was unconstitutional.

The country kept growing. More states wished to be added. On March 4, 1791, Vermont became the fourteenth state.

During 1791, Alexander Hamilton asked Congress to

create taxes to raise money to support the government. One of these was a high tax on the makers of whiskey— 25 percent of the selling price of each bottle. Farmers in the western territories objected. It was expensive to ship their wheat to the eastern cities. Instead, they distilled it into whiskey and sold that. Or they traded it for goods they needed on their farms. They grumbled about the excise tax for the next three years.

When Washington needed to discuss governmental matters and get advice, he met with each member of his Cabinet, one at a time. He received daily packets of information from them, keeping him abreast of each Cabinet member's doings. He would make comments or write questions that they would answer in writing a few days later.

They would not meet together as a group until November 26, 1791. He relied on his Cabinet for advice just as he did his war council during the Revolution. He thought long and hard about problems before he made his decision. In this way, he set the pattern for all Presidents.

On December 15, 1791, the Bill of Rights (the first ten amendments to the Constitution) Washington had requested in his inaugural address became law. It guaranteed basic liberties to the American people.

On April 2, 1792, Congress established a national mint in Philadelphia to print money for the new nation. Hamilton had put the government on a strong financial base. The new nation's money would be respected and would keep its value.

Washington only vetoed two Congressional bills during his two terms of office. His first veto occurred on April 5, 1792. His reason each time for vetoing the bills was that the proposed law would conflict with the Constitution.

The Bill of Rights was added to the Constitution in 1791.

Another state joined the union on June 1, 1792. Kentucky became the fifteenth state. Each time a state joined the nation, another stripe was added to the flag. Fifteen stripes made for a very large flag.

Work on the new capital of the United States progressed. On October 13, 1792, the cornerstone of the President's house was laid.

Hamilton and Jefferson continued to clash. In these conflicts, President Washington usually found himself leaning toward Hamilton's views. Hamilton's plans for industrialization of the country would assist strong economic growth. The creation of a national bank and protective tariffs on imported goods all assisted the development of industry and prosperity. Taxes, including excise taxes on whiskey, raised funds to meet government expenses.

Secretary of State Jefferson continued to oppose Hamilton's ways of gathering money for government expenses, his idea of a national bank, his plans to industrialize the nation, and most of his other ideas. Hamilton also offended Jefferson by moving into Jefferson's area of expertise. In 1793, he put pressure on the President to support the British against the French during a trade war.

The two men became so opposed to each other that Jefferson resigned in 1793, near the end of Washington's first term, rather than continue to work with Hamilton.

7

SECOND TERM

W ashington wished that all the members of his government would work together. However, by 1792, rival national parties began developing. They polarized around Jefferson and Hamilton. Hamilton's followers called themselves Federalists. They believed in strong national government. Washington kept choosing men with Federalist views to fill the positions in his Cabinet. He became known as a Federalist himself.

Jefferson's followers were known as Democratic-Republicans. This was the beginning of the modern Democratic party. Jeffersonians fought for the rights of the little people of the country—the farmers and workers. They tried to make sure these people were not trampled on by an uncaring government.

The Constitution did not say how many terms a President can serve. Washington almost set another precedent serving for one term. He intended to retire in 1793. However, he saw that if he did retire, the Union would be split by a bitter battle between the rival Hamiltonian and Jeffersonian factions. It might possibly even dissolve. He decided to remain in office for a second term.

Again he was elected unanimously on November 6, 1792. John Adams again came in second. Again Adams was Vice President. Washington's second inauguration was held on March 4, 1793, in the Senate Chamber of Federal Hall in Philadelphia. This inaugural address was even shorter than the first. It has remained the shortest inaugural address ever.

The very next month—on April 22, 1793— Washington issued a Neutrality Proclamation. This was to keep the United States out of the war between France and Great Britain. In it he advised the states to remain friendly with both sides (neutral in the conflict). He also warned them against getting involved in smuggling weapons to one side or the other. Congress followed in 1794 with a neutrality law.

On September 18, 1793, Washington visited the growing capital city on the Potomac. He laid the cornerstone of the United States Capitol building.

Meanwhile, opposition to the Whiskey Tax continued to fester. The protesters advanced from sending quiet petitions to Congress to burning the whiskey stills of those who paid this tax. In the summer of 1794, during a conflict between a tax collector and western Pennsylvania farmers calling themselves Whiskey Boys, several men were wounded. One man died.

The government could not ignore this violence. The Whiskey Rebellion became the first real test of federal power and unity. Washington issued a call for state militia troops. Four states responded with about fifteen thousand men.[1] He rode at the head of this huge contingent of men for the first two hundred miles. This was the first and last time that the President of the United States had led United States troops to battle in person.

Washington remained at Bedford, Pennsylvania. General Henry "Light Horse Harry" Lee took the troops to face the approximately five thousand rebelling farmers. However, when the militia arrived in western Pennsylvania, the rebels had fled. Of the handful of prisoners captured, only eighteen were tried. Only two of them were convicted of high treason against the nation.

The first presidential amnesty (pardon to insurrectionists) was issued on July 10, 1795. Washington granted a full pardon to the participants in the recent Whiskey Rebellion provided they signed an oath of allegiance to the United States.

This action may have seemed like taking an army to squash a flea. However, the show of federal force

SOURCE DOCUMENT

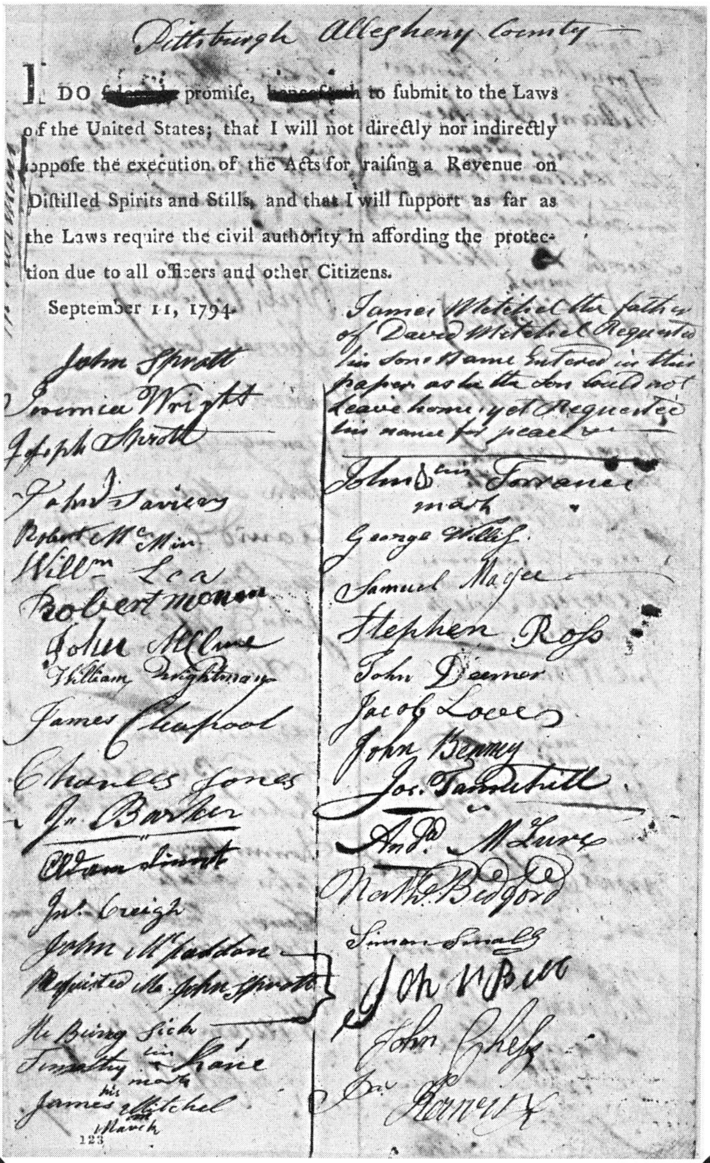

Pittsburgh Allegheny County

I DO ~~solemnly~~ promife, ~~henceforth~~ to fubmit to the Laws of the United States; that I will not directly nor indirectly oppofe the execution of the Acts for raifing a Revenue on Diftilled Spirits and Stills, and that I will fupport as far as the Laws require the civil authority in affording the protection due to all officers and other Citizens.

September 11, 1794.

[handwritten signatures, left column:]
John Sprott
Jeremiah Wright
Joseph Sprott
John Davies
Robert McMin
Willm Lea
Robert McnonN
John McClure
William Wrightman
James Claphool
Charles Jones
Jn Barker
Adam Sinnt
Jno Creigh
John McHaddon
Requested by John Sprott
He Being Sick
Timothy Kane
James Mitchel

[handwritten text, right column:]
James Mitchel the father of David Mitchel Requested his Sons Name Entered in this paper as he the son could not leave home yet Requested his name for peace

John Torrance
George Willes
Samuel Magee
Stephen Ross
John Deemer
Jacob Loee
John Benny
Jos. Tannihill
Andw McClure
North. Bedford
Simon Smalts
John McBell
John McKee

This oath of allegiance was signed by the members of the Whiskey Rebellion of 1794.

proved to the world and to the inhabitants of the country that the United States had merged into one unified country. It also showed that the laws were to be applied to all people within it. It showed that the federal government had the power to enforce its laws.

In the Northwest Territory another problem was caused by British soldiers remaining in forts there. They encouraged Native Americans to attack the American settlers in the area. This could have caused a war between Britain and the new country, but Washington prevented it by sending Chief Justice John Jay to negotiate a treaty (the Jay Treaty).

This was an unpopular move. Many people opposed any ties with the country's past enemy—Britain. Washington was attacked in the press. People shouted at him in the street.

However, Washington was determined to keep his country at peace. He signed the trade agreement with Great Britain on November 19, 1794. The agreement forced the British to remove themselves from their forts within the United States Northwest Territories.

However, in exchange, the treaty refused to recognize the United States' view of neutrality rights on the seas. This meant that any British ship had the right to board American ships and claim anything useful to them, including food and people they thought were British subjects. They forced the people they kidnapped to work aboard the British ships.

Washington protested this part of the treaty. However, in the end he signed it.

The Senate ratified the treaty in 1795. Then both the House of Representatives and the Senate had to vote money to implement the treaty. The House refused. They insisted they should have the right to participate in the making of the treaty, as well. When the House asked to examine all the papers in connection with the treaty, Washington refused. He thereby established the right of Presidents to resist congressional overviews of policy.

Another treaty in 1795, known as Pinckney's Treaty, was signed with Spain. It established the boundary between the United States and Spanish Florida at the thirty-first parallel. It also granted United States ships and people free access to the entire length of the Mississippi River. The port of New Orleans at the mouth of the river remained in Spanish hands. However, the treaty also insured free access to the port to let people sell their goods.

In 1795, the first hard-surfaced toll road in the United States was completed. It reached sixty-two miles from Philadelphia to Lancaster, Pennsylvania. This was a project dear to Alexander Hamilton's heart. The United States needed a good road system connecting the states, both for ease of communication and commerce. This was the first step.

On May 31, 1796, a treaty with the Six Native American Nations including delegates of the Great

Lakes, Mississippi River, and Ohio River tribes was signed. This effectively ended the Indian wars in the Northwest Territory. The Native Americans agreed to move out of the territory or leave settlers alone.

One more state joined the Union on June 1, 1796. Tennessee became the sixteenth state. No other states were created during Washington's time in office.

At the end of the second four years in office, Washington decided that two terms as President of the United States was enough. He refused to consider a third term. He wished to show that a President was not elected for life. A President should step aside and pass the power on to someone chosen in a free election.

This set a precedent of a two-term limit that all succeeding Presidents followed until the 1940s. Franklin Delano Roosevelt was elected President for four terms.

On September 17, 1796, George Washington published his Farewell Address in a Philadelphia newspaper. He also made it available to the press throughout the country. In the first paragraph he stated, "I should now apprise you of the resolution I have formed to decline being considered among the number of those out of whom a choice is to be made. . . ." for the office of President.[2]

He suggested the United States should attempt to remain neutral. They should avoid long-term alliances. They should stay out of European struggles as much as possible. America continued his policy of isolationism for the next one hundred years.

The address went on to advise against the evils of political parties. However, he failed in his attempt to stop the rise of opposing political parties. The next election was a bitter one. Thomas Jefferson, with Aaron Burr as his chosen Vice President, ran against the Federalist John Adams and Thomas Pinckney.

This was the first election to be contested by party candidates. However, there was no primary election to nominate them, nor a national convention. By letters and private conferences, political leaders of the day chose the men to run for office.

The campaign was a rough one. It turned Adams and Jefferson into sworn enemies. Mud was thrown by both sides. Jefferson's Democratic-Republicans accused Adams of wanting to be a king in America. The Federalists countered by calling Jefferson a demagogue—a manipulator of fear to get political power.

When the electoral college met and voted, a shocking thing happened. Adams received the most votes. However, Jefferson came in a close second. Jefferson became Adams' Vice President! Two men directly opposed to each other in policy and thought were now tied together.

The other amazing thing about this election was the result. Despite the angry words during the election, after election day the reins of government had been peacefully passed to another.

Jefferson accepted his post as Vice President. He did not propose a rebellion. He and his party did not resort to violence or plot to take over the government. Instead, everyone worked within the system. They resolved to try harder during the next election to win the post for their own party.

An amendment was added to the Constitution in 1804. This Twelfth Amendment provided that the President of the United States and his Vice President must be elected separately. Never again would they be of opposing parties.

George Washington, now a retired citizen, attended John Adams' inauguration alone. However, when the crowd caught sight of him, they cheered.

8

A WELL-EARNED RETIREMENT

In 1797, the sixty-five-year-old George Washington retired, again, to Mount Vernon. The population of the United States had grown to about 4.9 million people.[1]

Although he had adopted and had helped raise Martha's children, he and Martha had no children together. He was a father, however. Since he had made certain that the rules of government laid down by the constitution worked, he is considered the Father of His Country.

At long last Washington was able to remove himself from public life and concentrate on improving his Mount Vernon. He received no pension from the government. Retirement benefits for government officials did not begin until the twentieth century. He needed money to continue living in the way he and Martha had become accustomed. He sold off some of his land in western Virginia.

Martha Washington was delighted to be home again with just the family, away from the political scene.[2] Washington shared her pleasure.

He immersed himself in plantation life. In his daily rides around the property, he oversaw the production on his land. He planned improvements to his land and buildings. Some of the wood in Mount Vernon itself had rotted and needed to be replaced. In the evenings he

Washington directing the management of his farms. (From a painting by J.B. Stearns.)

Martha Dandridge Custis Washington (1731–1802).

relaxed at home. He often read newspapers aloud in the evening to his wife.

However, he could not escape public life. Thousands of people came to visit him. Many were friends. At times, perfect strangers stopped by just to stare at him and his family.[3]

They came because Washington had issued an invitation to the people of the United States to visit him. He said, "I have no objection to any sober or orderly person's gratifying their curiosity in viewing the buildings, Gardens, &ca. About Mount Vernon."[4]

(Mount Vernon has been preserved by a private society called the Mount Vernon Ladies' Association of the Union. The house and grounds are open to the public every day of the year. More than 50 million have visited it since it was opened in 1858.)

Even though he had retired, he kept in touch with the government. At one point, tension became so great between France and the United States that there was talk of war. President Adams asked Washington to become lieutenant-general and commander-in-chief of all the armies. He accepted in July 1798. Washington was the only former President to hold such a post.

He spent the next year choosing his general staff. Fortunately, the United States was never invaded. All the battles in this undeclared struggle between the two countries were by ships at sea. A treaty was eventually signed in 1800 ending the struggle. But Washington did not live long enough to see this treaty.

On December 12, 1799, Washington took his usual horseback ride around his farmland beginning at 10:00 A.M. He rode through snow, hail, and later a cold rain. Since darkness comes early in December, he returned to Mount Vernon by 3:00 P.M. Without changing his wet clothing, he ate dinner. Later that evening he complained of a sore throat.

The next day, doctors were called. They decided he had inflammatory quinsy, another name for a severe form of tonsillitis. They attempted several treatments, including bleeding and plasters. This was the usual procedure in those days. Antibiotics had not been discovered yet. However, his tonsils grew larger and larger. Soon Washington could not swallow any medicine.

He had survived all the childhood diseases that had killed several of his brothers and sisters. As an adult he had lived through fevers, smallpox, dysentery, and various bouts with flu. He had survived surgery for a

This is the tomb at Mount Vernon where George and Martha Washington are buried.

large tumor on his thigh in 1789. He had a lighthearted contempt for medical men. Washington often told them to "Let it go as it came."[5] However, he could not survive being choked by his own tonsils. He died on December 14, 1799. Martha remained by his side until the end.

Martha Washington died on May 22, 1802, just before her seventy-first birthday. They are both buried in the family tomb on the grounds of Mount Vernon.

For months the entire nation mourned George Washington. General Henry "Light Horse Harry" Lee gave a funeral oration for George Washington before the house of Congress on December 26, 1799. In it he declared that Washington was, ". . . first in war, first in peace, and first in the hearts of his countrymen."[6]

9

WASHINGTON'S LEGACY

W ashington learned as a young boy about honor and duty. For the rest of his life he tried to live up to the high standards he set for himself. These qualities brought him to the forefront in the major American events of the eighteenth century. He became one of the founders of the United States of America. He was the first President elected under the new Constitution.

Among his friends he showed his sense of humor, enjoying racy jokes and ironies.[1] To the general public, however, he turned a sterner face. As general and commander-in-chief of the army of the United Colonies and later as President, he felt he should act with formality and ceremony to create respect for the office, if not for the man in the office.[2] His height and impressive bearing helped him carry this off. Also his manner of being a slow but careful thinker added to his dignity.

Legends rose about the possibility that he may not have smiled because of bad teeth. It is true that his teeth became so bad that most of them were removed. But it is not true that his false teeth were made of wood. He had several sets made from lead or gold with teeth carved from ivory or the tusk of the hippopotamus. A few of his own teeth were also placed in the frame.

Unfortunately, the art of dental work was not as comfortable then as now. His false teeth did not fit well. Nor did the hinges open and close very well. This led to his inability to make long speeches because of a tendency to mumble. He was also careful not to smile in public.

Both George and Martha Washington insisted on ceremony while Washington was President. At first, Washington was bothered by visitors who tried to interrupt him all the time. Therefore, he established Tuesday receptions for men only. He also stated that he would receive visiting dignitaries only between 2:00 P.M. and 3:00 P.M., two days a week. This gave him space to handle the chores of government without interruption on other days.

Evening receptions were more relaxed, although they were still quite formal by today's standards. The ladies were invited to these events. Martha Washington ran these.

People called Martha Washington 'Lady Washington' as if she were of European nobility.[3] This led to the habit of referring to the President's wife as the First Lady of the land.

Washington established that the office of President was to be respected over the governors of states early in his presidency. At one point he visited Massachusetts. Governor John Hancock discovered he could not force the President to go visit him. Instead Hancock had to call on the President.

Until the invention of the special security automobile (the first one was bought for President William Howard Taft), presidential coaches were not supplied by the country. They either came out of the President's own pocket or were gifts.

Washington's preference for a plain and elegant style was ignored. The government of Pennsylvania donated a cream-colored carriage. It was decorated with Washington's crest and oval panels painted with the four seasons. It was called the Penn Coach. Six white horses pulled it. For travel, however, the President and his family used his own sturdy traveling coach.

Buttons made in honor of George Washington's first inauguration in 1789 may be the ancestors of today's campaign buttons. Several designs exist. One button was embossed with an eagle. Another showed his initials and the words, "Long Live the President."

In Washington's honor, one state, thirty-three

counties, seven mountains, and nine colleges were named after him.[4]

Many cities and private organizations raised monuments to honor him. Most were tall piles of stone, but one is different. A representation of his head is carved onto Mount Rushmore.

He has been honored by the Treasury Department, also. His face is both on the quarter and the dollar bill, two items constantly in use.

He is not remembered for being a great general and battlefield tactician. However, he excelled as a great military leader and administrator who learned from his mistakes.

He went on to apply the diplomatic skills he learned in the military camps to running the new country. And yet he also prevented the army from becoming a force in politics. When he learned that some army members were thinking of using the army to force the country to accept him as king, he nipped the plan in the bud.

He used his influence and prestige to help swing the Constitutional Convention away from simply repairing the Articles of Confederation. He supported the writing of the new Constitution. This influenced the majority of the American people to accept this new type of government.

His bad teeth and deliberate thinking prevented him from being a gifted orator. However, that same deliberate thinking helped him keep control over the hotheads in his administration. He refused to react instantly to

The Washington Monument overlooks the reflecting pool and the Japanese cherry trees in Washington, D.C. It is 555 feet tall.

their demands. In this way, he managed to keep the United States neutral and safe for the twenty or more years he estimated the country needed to become a powerful nation.[5] Thanks to him, the new United States got that time.

His own dignity and honesty inspired nationwide

The huge carving on Mount Rushmore in the Black Hills of South Dakota features George Washington, Thomas Jefferson, Theodore Roosevelt, and Abraham Lincoln. Each head is sixty feet tall. The carving was begun in 1927 by Gutzon Borglum and finished by his son in 1941.

A replica of the United States one dollar bill. The picture is from a painting of the older George Washington done by Stuart.

and worldwide confidence in the new head of government. He worked within the constitutional powers of the presidency, although he defined them and enlarged them wherever necessary.

He gathered men of genius to advise him, even if they held conflicting views.

He brought the country from near financial ruin to financial stability. By the time he stepped down, the United States of America was respected throughout the civilized world for its integrity and competence.

President Washington's decisions during the last part of his second term were openly criticized by the Democratic-Republicans. Although personally offended by the remarks, he made certain that criticism would not be considered treason in the United States.

And finally, he oversaw the peaceful transition of power from one President to the next one. No longer would kings rule for life. Here in the United States the rulers had a limited term of office. They could be voted out by the people they ruled. They could retire peaceably.

Abigail Adams, the wife of President John Adams, told her sister after Washington's death that he:

> . . . never grew giddy, but ever maintained a modest diffidence of his own talents. . . . Possessed of power, possessed of an extensive influence, he never used it but for the benefit of his country. . . . If we look through the whole tenor of his life, history will not produce to us a parallel.[6]

George Washington Masonic National Memorial in Arlington, Virginia, just outside of Washington, D.C.

Chronology

1732—Born at Pope's Creek plantation, Virginia, on February 22.

1743—Augustine Washington (his father) dies; George inherits Ferry Farm and some town lots in Fredericksburg.

1748—First major surveying job in the Shenandoah.

1749—Becomes official surveyor for Culpeper County.

1752—Lawrence Washington (his half brother) dies; takes over his militia post.

1753—Delivers Governor Dinwiddie's ultimatum to the French in the Ohio Territory.

1754—Begins French and Indian War; attempts to build a fort and defend it from the French ending in surrender; joins the staff of General Edward Braddock.

1755—Braddock dies; Washington survives with four bullet holes through his coat and two horses shot under him; becomes commander of all the Virginia forces.

1758—Participates in expedition against Fort Duquesne (near Pittsburgh); is elected burgess for Frederick County; resigns militia commission in December.

1759—Marries Martha Dandridge Custis on January 6; adds a full second floor to Mount Vernon.

1761—Lawrence Washington's widow dies, leaving Mount Vernon to George Washington.

1775—Virginia delegate to Second Continental Congress; is elected general and commander-in-chief of the Army of the Continental Congress.

1776—Declaration of Independence is signed and read to all troops.

1781—Accepts surrender of Cornwallis, October 19.

1783—Resigns commission before Congress at Annapolis, Maryland.

1787—Attends convention to change the Articles of Confederation; is elected president of the Constitutional Convention.

1789—Is unanimously elected President of the United States; is inaugurated at New York City on April 30; mother dies August 25.

1790—Philadelphia becomes temporary capital of the United States.

1792—Is unanimously reelected President.

1793—Is inaugurated for second term of presidency at Philadelphia on March 4; lays cornerstone of the Capitol building in the new Federal city of Washington, D.C., on September 18.

1796—Washington's Farewell Address is published in the Philadelphia *Daily American Advertiser*, September 17.

1797—Retires.

1798—Is appointed lieutenant-general and commander-in-chief of the Armies of the United States.

1799—Dies at Mount Vernon on December 14 and is buried in the family vault there in December. A more substantial tomb is built years later.

Chapter Notes

Chapter 1

1. Robert F. Jones, *George Washington* (Boston: Twayne Publishers, 1979), p. 86.

2. Paul F. Boller, Jr., *Presidential Anecdotes* (New York: Oxford University Press, 1981), p. 13.

3. Ibid., p. 14.

4. Joseph Nathan Kane, *Facts About the Presidents* (New York: H.W. Wilson, Co., 1981), p. 11.

5. Jones, p. 87.

6. Ibid., p. 86.

7. Frank Freidel, "George Washington: First President 1789–1797," *National Geographic*, November 1964, p. 657.

8. John R. Alden, *George Washington: A Biography* (Baton Rouge, La.: Louisiana State University Press, 1984), p. 236.

9. Ibid.

10. Washington Irving, *George Washington: A Biography* (Garden City, N.Y.: Doubleday & Company, 1976), p. 652.

11. Jones, p. 88.

Chapter 2

1. William A. Degregorio, *The Complete Book of U.S. Presidents* (New York: Dembner Books, 1984), p. 3.

2. Ibid., p. 2.

3. Suzanne Hilton, *The World of Young George Washington* (New York: Walker & Co., 1987), p. 43.

4. *World Book of America's Presidents, Volume 2—Portraits of the Presidents* (Chicago, Ill.: World Book, 1994), p. 15.

5. John E. Ferling, *The First of Men: A Life of George Washington* (Knoxville, Tenn.: The University of Tennessee Press, 1988), p. 6.

6. Robert F. Jones, *George Washington* (Boston: Twayne Publishers, 1979), p. 15.

7. Frank Freidel, "George Washington, First President 1789–1797," *National Geographic*, November 1964, p. 646.

8. Jones, p. 17.

9. Ibid., p. 18.

Chapter 3

1. Robert F. Jones, *George Washington* (Boston: Twayne Publishers, 1979), p. 21.

2. Frank Freidel, "George Washington, First President 1789–1797," *National Geographic*, November 1964, p. 648.

3. William A. Degregorio, *The Complete Book of U.S. Presidents* (New York: Dembner Books, 1984), p.5.

4. Ibid., p. 4.

5. Jones, p. 25.

6. John E. Ferling, *The First of Men: A Life of George Washington* (Knoxville, Tenn.: The University of Tennessee Press, 1988), p. 52.

7. Richard Norton Smith, *Patriarch—George Washington and the New American Nation* (Boston: Houghton Mifflin Company, 1993), p. xviii.

8. Charles Wall, *Mount Vernon: a Handbook* (Mount Vernon, Va.: The Mount Vernon Ladies' Association of the Union, 1985), p. 21.

9. Ibid., p. 14.

Chapter 4

1. John E. Ferling, *The First of Men: A Life of George Washington* (Knoxville, Tenn.: The University of Tennessee Press, 1988), p. 170.

2. William A. Degregorio, *The Complete Book of U.S. Presidents* (New York: Dembner Books, 1984), p. 5.

3. Samuel Eliot Morison and Henry Steele Commager, *The Growth of the American Republic,* Volume 1 (New York: Oxford University Press, 1962), p. 181.

4. Robert F. Jones, *George Washington* (Boston: Twayne Publishers, 1979), p. 42.

5. Morison and Commager, p. 184.

6. John R. Alden, *George Washington: A Biography* (Baton Rouge, La.: Louisiana State University Press, 1984), p. 113.

7. Jones, p. 45.

8. Ferling, p. 285.

Chapter 5

1. Paul F. Boller, Jr., *Presidential Anecdotes* (New York: Oxford University Press, 1981), p. 15.

2. John R. Alden, *George Washington: A Biography* (Baton Rouge, La.: Louisiana State University Press, 1984), p. 210.

3. Frank Freidel, "George Washington, First President 1789–1797," *National Geographic*, November 1964, p. 651.

4. Washington Irving, *George Washington: A Biography* (Garden City, N.Y.: Doubleday & Company, 1976), p. 640.

5. Richard M. Pious, *The Young Oxford Companion to the Presidency of the United States* (New York: Oxford University Press, 1994), p. 58.

6. Barry Schwartz, *George Washington: the Making of an American Symbol* (New York: Free Press, 1987), p. 47.

Chapter 6

1. Frank Freidel, "George Washington, First President 1789–1797," *National Geographic*, November 1964, p. 653.

2. Robert F. Jones, *George Washington* (Boston: Twayne Publishers, 1979), p. 90.

3. David C. Whitney, *The American Presidents* (Garden City, N.Y.: Doubleday & Company, 1978), p. 23.

4. John R. Alden, *George Washington: A Biography* (Baton Rouge, La.: Louisiana State University Press, 1984), p. 236.

5. Ibid.

6. Ibid.

7. Freidel, p. 654.

8. *World Book of America's Presidents, Volume 2—Portraits of the Presidents* (Chicago, Ill.: World Book, 1994), p. 23.

Chapter 7

1. William A. Degregorio, *The Complete Book of U.S. Presidents* (New York: Dembner Books, 1984), p. 10.

2. Joseph Nathan Kane, *Facts About the Presidents* (New York: H.W. Wilson, Co., 1981), p. 16.

Chapter 8

1. *World Book of America's Presidents, Volume 2—Portraits of the Presidents* (Chicago, Ill.: World Book, 1994), p. 23.

2. Ibid., p. 22.

3. William A. Degregorio, *The Complete Book of U.S. Presidents* (New York: Dembner Books, 1984), p. 13.

4. Charles Wall, *Mount Vernon: a Handbook* (Mount Vernon, Va.: The Mount Vernon Ladies' Association of the Union, 1985), p. 25.

5. Richard Norton Smith, *Patriarch—George Washington and the New American Nation* (Boston: Houghton Mifflin Company, 1993), p. xiv.

6. Frank Freidel, "George Washington, First President 1789–1797," *National Geographic*, November 1964, p. 646.

Chapter 9

1. John R. Alden, *George Washington: A Biography* (Baton Rouge, La.: Louisiana State University Press, 1984), p. 304.

2. Frank Freidel, "George Washington, First President 1789–1797," *National Geographic*, November 1964, p. 656.

3. Robert F. Jones, *George Washington* (Boston: Twayne Publishers, 1979), p. 90.

4. Richard Norton Smith, *Patriarch—George Washington and the New American Nation* (Boston: Houghton Mifflin Company, 1993), p. xix.

5. Freidel, p. 656.

6. Ibid., p. 657.

Further Reading

Hilton, Suzanne. *The World of Young George Washington*. New York: Walker and Company, 1987.

Jones, Robert F. *George Washington*. Boston: Twayne Publishers, 1979.

Judson, Karen. *The Constitution of the United States*. Springfield, NJ: Enslow Publishers, 1996.

Judson, Karen. *The Presidency of the United States*. Springfield, NJ: Enslow Publishers, 1996.

Kent, Zachary. *George Washington: First President of the United States*. Chicago: Children's Press, 1986.

Meltzer, Milton. *George Washington and the Birth of Our Nation*. New York: Franklin Watts, 1986.

Minks, Benton and Louise. *The French and Indian War*. San Diego, CA: Lucent Books, 1995.

Morris, Jeffrey. *Great Presidential Decisions—The Washington Way*. Minneapolis: Lerner Publications, 1994.

Smith, Carter, ed. *The Revolutionary War: A Sourcebook on Colonial America*. Brookfield, CT: The Millbrook Press, 1991.

Stokesbury, James. *A Short History of the American Revolution*. New York: William Morrow and Company, 1991.

Internet Addresses

Home page for Mount Vernon

http://www.mountvernon.org

The Declaration of Independence

http://www.cs.indiana.edu/statecraft/decl.html

Historical and modern political documents (Among these are the United States Constitution and the Declaration of Independence)

http://www.cs.indiana.edu/inds/politics.html

Home page for Williamsburg Online

http://www.gc.net/wol/wol.html

Colonial Williamsburg home page

http://www.history.org

Short articles about each President

http://www.whitehouse.gov/WH/glimpse/presidents/html/presidents.html

The Washington Monument in Washington, D.C. (information plus all four views of the city from the top of the monument)

http://www.nps.gov/wamo/index2.htm

Biography of George Washington (It links to information about the Washington Memorial and a map of downtown Washington, D.C.)

http://sc94.ameslab.gov/TOUR/gwash.html

Index